D0283641

The Religion of
PRESIDENT CARTER

by
Niels C. Nielsen, Jr.

THOMAS NELSON INC., PUBLISHERS
Nashville ● New York

Copyright © 1977 by Niels C. Nielsen, Jr.

All rights reserved under International and Pan-American Conventions.
Published by Thomas Nelson, Inc., Publishers, Nashville, Tennessee
Manufactured in the United States of America

ISBN 0-8407-5621-6

Contents

Preface

BIOGRAPHY

Jimmy Carter was inaugurated January 20, 1977, as the thirty-ninth president of the United States of America. The first Southerner to occupy the White House since Zachary Taylor, a hundred and twenty-eight years earlier, Carter's rise to prestige and fame has been rapid and sudden. A dozen months before taking the oath of office on an open Bible, President Carter was virtually unknown. Campaigning far and wide for more than a year, his charisma was beginning to be felt. One of the ways his religion became known was through his comments about prayer. "I don't pray to God to let me win an election," he said. "I pray to ask God to let me do the right thing."[1] The reasons for the president's success as well as the role of religion in his private and public life have been widely discussed. Analysis must necessarily include his autobiography, *Why Not the Best?*, published by the Southern Baptist Broadman Press.[2]

EXTERNAL HISTORY

President Carter, born October 1, 1924, has two younger sisters and one brother. One sister, Ruth Carter Stapleton, is now an evangelist. His brother, Billy, thirteen years his junior, is in charge of the family peanut business. The president's mother, Lillian, an outspoken person, is a registered nurse, who has served both blacks and whites in the community of Plains, Georgia. "I go to church on Sunday," she has said, "but I don't think all churchgoers are Christians. I think there's a difference between religion and Christianity."[3] After her husband died in July of 1953, a victim of cancer, she volunteered for the Peace Corps at the age of sixty-eight and worked in India.

Jimmy's character was molded by the stern discipline of his father for whom he had both respect and affection, but he believes his life was influenced more by his mother. He learned his reading habits from her, and she was more liberal than his father on the issue of race. In his autobiography, the president also mentions the influence of the Plains High School superintendent, Miss Julia Coleman. When he was only twelve, she called him in and recommended that he read Tolstoy's *War and Peace*. It convinced him of the predominant role of the common, ordinary people in history.

In Plains there was social stability. "Jimmy Carter believes that one can go home again; he always has."[4] The president describes the integrity of life among his people: "You know, when things started going wrong in my own life, my mother and father were there, and my sisters and brother were there, and the church was there. . . ." The community was there, and it never did change and has not yet. "There was something around which I built my life."[5]

The Carters had settled in Plains, Georgia, by the 1830s. Protestants, they became cotton merchants and landowners. Following the defeat of the Confederacy, they planted peanuts as a cash crop. Jimmy's father owned an extensive spread of land and operated a general store at one end of the town. Concentrated effort and hard work were required to remain above the subsistence level. The Carter home had no running water or electricity until Franklin Roosevelt's program of rural electrification. Nevertheless, the family was not considered poor. As many as thirty dependent families of blacks worked for Mr. Earl, Jimmy's father.

INTERNAL HISTORY

The president's religious symbols and values were shaped in this milieu. In addition to his external history, his internal, personal history is important for the evaluation of his character and faith. As early as the age of five he said he wished to attend the Naval Academy at Annapolis. His purpose was encouraged by the letters from his mother's brother, a Navy radioman who visited many foreign ports. Since Mr. Earl had been active in politics, he was able to secure the needed appointment for his son without difficulty. Midshipman Carter graduated in the upper ten percent of his class in 1946. That summer, he married Rosalynn Smith in the Plains Methodist Church. Her ambition and political judgment have been indispensable to her husband's political career. She also shares his religion.

Jimmy Carter's self-image was once shaken by Admiral Hyman Rickover, who was interviewing him for the nuclear submarine program. The two men sat in a large room by themselves. Rickover let the young officer choose his own subjects—current events, seamanship, music, literature, naval tactics, electronics, gunnery. Then Rickover asked a series of questions of increasing difficulty. "He always looked right into my eyes," Carter remembers, "and he never smiled. I was saturated with cold sweat."[6]

At last Rickover asked how the officer had stood in his class at Annapolis. Fifty-ninth in a class of 820 was the answer, expecting the usual congratulations. But Rickover asked, "Did you do your best?" When Carter had to admit that he did not always do his best, Rickover closed the interview with ''Why not?'' Shaken, the young officer slowly left the room.

Rickover was in part a substitute father figure. Carter writes: ''We feared and respected him and strove to please him. The absence of comment was his compliment. He expected the maximum from us, but he always contributed more.''[7] The future president accepted the Admiral's ideal of perfection and stern responsibility. He states that Admiral Rickover probably affected his life more profoundly than anyone other than his parents.

However, Jimmy Carter decided to resign from the Navy and return home to Plains when his father died of cancer in 1953.

He took over the family business. It was a time of crisis and re-evaluation. Rosalynn did not want to return to the small town. The family farm was not prosperous, and the first years were difficult financially.

FROM PLAINS TO THE PRESIDENCY

Jimmy participated in local service club activities, school politics, and the Plains Baptist Church. Asked to join the White Citizens' Council by the local Baptist minister, he refused, ignoring threats and a short-lived boycott of his business. In fact, he was among the very few persons who openly opposed the continuing segregation of his church.

In 1962, Carter was elected to the Georgia State Senate and served two terms. He won in his second campaign for governor of Georgia. In this office, he was visited by the majority of presidential hopefuls.

The governor was not impressed by their abilities and decided that he could do just as well or better. His decision to run for the presidency, first made known to his cousin, State Sen. Hugh Carter, has been told in typical Carter lore.

Jimmy went to Hugh's house and knocked at the back door. "Hugh," Jimmy said, "I want to talk to you." They went into the den, and Jimmy continued: "I've got something to tell you, and I want all the family to know it first: I'm going to run for president of the United States."[8]

Hugh looked at his relative a little in awe and said, "Jimmy, you mean that?" "Yes, I do," came the reply.

Later, Hugh offered this advice: "If you do not want to vote for the man, stay away from him. Because if he talks to you, you will feel the sincerity in him. Before you know it, you will be telling him about your life."

On November 4, 1972, just a day before Richard Nixon's landslide victory over George McGovern, Carter's aide, Hamilton Jordon, drew up a careful campaign plan.[9] The governor accepted Jordon's judgment that the chief issue in the next presidential election would be character more than domestic or foreign policy. Three years later, following this idea, Carter entered thirty of thirty-one primaries. He campaigned energetically day and night and won enough votes for the nomination even before the Democratic Convention. "Our strategy was simple," he explained, "make a total effort all over the nation."[10] The fact is that he ran against everybody in the primaries and won. In Madison Square Garden, the Democratic Party confirmed his victory over every established politician. The candidate chose Walter Mondale as his vice presidential running mate, a choice that may have brought the margin of victory.

CARTER AS A CHRISTIAN

Jimmy Carter planned carefully, worked continually, and remained ambitious and self-confident. As a Christian, he could take time to discuss the "I am third" process with

Tom Whitney, even while campaigning. Whitney was the young Democratic state chairman in Iowa. ''God is first, family and friends are second, and I am third.''[11]

Carter was not just making politics. He was serious, trying to say to Whitney what it means to love one's neighbor. The candidate's sensitivity for persons was typified when he collected arrowheads from his farm, to send to the fatally ill daughter of a reporter who traveled on his plane.

It has been said that John F. Kennedy proved that a Roman Catholic can be elected president of the United States. Jimmy Carter has shown that an openly professing, twice-born Christian can come to the highest office in the land. His religious image, expressed in humility, and the acknowledged need for forgiveness enhanced his candidacy. He has tried to explain that he is not an inflexible moralist who refuses all compromise. To say the least, he takes note of contexts and circumstances as any successful politician must do. He worked for a maximum of political power. As president, he assuredly will be his own man in both politics and religion.

EVALUATION

The enigma of Jimmy Carter! Repeated and exaggerated emphasis was given to that theme when the Georgian broke into public view. Is Carter's religion also an enigma? This book has been written on the premise that it is not, and that sufficient materials are available to delimit the main outlines of the president's religion. Reluctantly at first, and then in repeated interviews, Carter expressed his religious views and what his religion means to him. The background and setting can be identified. To be sure, Carter's faith is a living thing—not formal or static. Fresh nuances and expression may evoke surprise—as in the *Playboy* interview.

Preface

But what the president believes about God, humankind, and the world need not be in doubt.

In appraising Carter's religion, excessive eulogy is of as little help as skeptical rejection. Neither serves to explain the subtleties of his position or psychology. Empathy and sympathetic understanding—not merely criticism from without—are the intention of this writing. We have not attempted to treat all sides of the thirty-ninth president's career and politics. Our interest is not so much to say what will be forthcoming in his presidency—a question which cannot be avoided—as simply to understand how he thinks about religion.

The "Carter phenomenon" is fascinating and intriguing.

There are obvious dangers in writing about a leader who is so new to the Washington scene, so much an outsider. Time and history alone will tell how he will stand up to the pressures attendant to the role of president, and whether his religious faith can make any significant contribution to his term in office. Carter's interest in religion is not primarily speculative. Our analysis seeks to avoid imposing contrived categories on his thought. A practicing politician of notable skill, he put together a remarkable election coalition. If his combination of ambition and piety is dissolved, we no longer have the vital leader he has shown himself to be.

SEQUENCE OF CHAPTERS

This book begins with questions about the president's religion as they have appeared in public opinion. The second chapter is an attempt to place him, not only as a Christian but a Southern Baptist. His high office is heavy with symbolism. The religions of the presidents will be discussed in the third chapter. In the belief that Carter's election would have been unlikely if not impossible without the shadow of Watergate, the fourth chapter considers how this crisis raised the question of religion, together with the issue of presidential character. The fifth and sixth chapters deal with Carter's stance on two specific problems, race and international relations. Other areas could have been selected, but these two were chosen because they illustrate both his psychology and moral principles. The seventh chapter takes on the generally misunderstood *Playboy* interview and attempts to appraise its religious bases. Is Carter an evangelical? What is his relation to Roman Catholics and Jews? These matters are discussed before the concluding chapter returns to the problem of presidential character, and a detailed appraisal of the president's conversion experience.

ACKNOWLEDGMENTS

A number of persons who have shared Jimmy Carter's faith have provided information for this book. I am especially indebted to Jack Harwell, editor of the *Baptist Index* in Atlanta, who is succeeding Carter as a member of the Brotherhood Mission Board. His own first-hand knowledge was helpful in confirming a number of the theses of this book, and he also introduced me to other Southern Baptist clergy who have known the Carter family. My colleague in the department of religious studies at Rice University, Prof. John Newport, a Southern Baptist, read the manuscript of this book. Although he supplied a number of helpful suggestions for revision, he is not responsible for my judgments. We both teach at a secular, private university which is not church affiliated. Although this book appraises the phenomenon of Carter's religion positively, it also calls attention to a number of points which invite further discussion. Its purpose is to highlight ideas and problems, not to offer an apologetic.

The Religion of
PRESIDENT
CARTER

1. Questions about Carter's Religion

IS IT "FOR REAL"?

Seldom, if ever, has a presidential candidate been so scrutinized for his personal religious convictions. The question keeps coming up: Is Carter a "phony"?

"Of course, he is. He is a politician, an actor, a salesman," wrote Richard Reeves in the *New York* magazine before Carter's nomination.[1] "What I like is that the product he's peddling is one of the most interesting I've seen in a long time." Reeves went on to describe the candidate as a Southern Populist, free of the race anchor, a man who has outgrown his origins and repackaged the salable points of his life and public record—something of a 1976 Huey Long. Contrary to Reeves, the majority of news people have not charged that Carter is a phony.

The Pulitzer Prize winning novelist and essayist Norman Mailer visited Plains before the election and observed that Carter was quiet in his charisma. "It was as if he knew that God had given him intelligence and good work that would make sense."[2] Carter could give his strength to the world and get new strength back. Mailer explained the famous Carter smile. He said it came with the quiet pleasure of

17

possessing a piece of the cosmos that Carter knew was his, and was as natural as the odor of resin coming off a pine. Mailer concluded that Jimmy Carter was "somewhere within range of the very good and very decent man he presented himself to be." Mailer thought he would be happy to vote for such a man on election day. "After all, it was not every day that you could pull the lever for a man whose favorite song was 'Amazing Grace, how sweet the sound that saved a wretch like me—I once was lost, but now I'm found, was blind but now I see.' "

An official of the Kennedy Institute of Politics at Harvard thought otherwise: "I would never vote for anyone who believed in God."[3] Carter has said, "If there are those who don't want to vote for me because I'm a deeply committed Christian, I believe they should vote for someone else."[4] The historian James T. Baker describes Carter as "essentially a new phenomenon in American politics."[5] Of all the thirty-seven Protestant and one Roman Catholic Presidents, Carter is the first to have a fully developed "salvationist" theology. No president in this century, perhaps since the beginning of the Republic, has talked so much in detail about his Christian experience. "My religion is as natural to me as breathing," he has said. Carter is explicit:

> I'm a father and I'm a Christian; I'm a businessman and I'm a Christian; I'm a farmer and I'm a Christian; I'm a politician and I'm a Christian. The most important thing in my life beyond all else is Jesus Christ. I think I've been made more aware of his influence in my life when I've had added this tremendous responsibility.[6]

Carter's organizational ability and eloquence have been nurtured by his Baptist background. He was baptized by immersion in 1935, having reached "the age of accountability." In an interview, Miss Lillian explained that the church is the center of everything in a small town. Plains didn't even have a beer joint at that time. A church and a school—that's all there was. Customarily, when a boy or girl became eleven or twelve, "they kind of get together. And they join the Baptist church together." It's not so much a religious experience as just a custom to be baptized. "And then they float merrily on."[7] Carter's experience of a more profound "new birth" came later in life. "I never did have a personal feeling of intimacy with Christ until, I'd say, ten, twelve years ago, and then I began to see much more clearly the significance of Christ in my life, and it changed my attitudes dramatically."

The former Roman Catholic seminarian, now a columnist, Garry Wills pondered: "It may seem unjust to punish real religion when we reward empty religiosity."[8] But he concluded that in Carter's case it could make sense. "A man who *means* what he says in this 'awesome area' drifts outside the ties and shared weaknesses that keep us in touch with each other." Carter has not been so punished by the majority of his fellow citizens. Electing him, they seem to believe his religion is not political but a highly personal and living commitment.

At first, Carter appeared reluctant to express his religious beliefs. But pressed with questions during the primary campaign, Carter refused to deny his conviction:

> When the media began to emphasize my beliefs, I did not know how to deal with it; whether to answer the questions or to say I didn't have a comment. I decided to tell the truth.[9]

SEPARATION OF CHURCH AND STATE

Personal religious experience is one thing, the achievement of love or justice in society another. Often, it is all too easy to identify a wide gap between piety and performance among politicians. Religious men have not always realized that their high ideals to commend brotherhood and righteousness in general terms does not necessarily give them a place in public life. The statesmen who wrote the Constitution of the United States of America were keenly aware that some honest unbelievers are more responsible than other persons who are religious bigots. They had seen piety used as a mask for tyranny in established churches, and they concluded that no real benefit comes to a commonwealth when faith is imposed from above. On this premise, the Founding Fathers fully disavowed the old union of throne and altar, erecting a wall of separation between church and state. A New Testament proof text could be, ''Render unto Caesar that which is Caesar's and to God that which is God's.''[10]

In fact, the claims of church and state have often been mixed throughout human history: in holy war, persecution, and intolerance. Such practice has debased high religion's role in reinforcing morality and critical judgment, and enriching human life.

In a century which has known Mussolini, Hitler, and Stalin as well as Woodrow Wilson, Franklin Roosevelt, Albert Schweitzer, Ghandi, and Churchill, the public has been conditioned to the appearance of fresh dramatic figures. Still, Carter has been something of a surprise. He has come on the scene, claiming that religion is important for his own life and that of others. He reportedly reads the Bible daily, believing it is true and reveals the nature of Deity, humankind, and the world. In Carter's philosophy of life, the human person is not alone in the universe. Nor is man an end in himself as is alleged in secular thought. Carter learns from the Bible that history is a mixture of good and evil. His reading of it evokes humility together with a sense of moral responsibility. What other statesmen and national leaders perceive as a political crisis, Carter understands to be largely a spiritual one.

THE PRESIDENT'S PRAYER AND WORSHIP

Alexander Solzhenitsyn, like Carter, also finds life's ultimate answer in Christianity. Solzhenitsyn recounts a meeting with a young Jewish prisoner.[11] In the hands of the police and still a Communist, Solzhenitsyn had read one of the prayers that President Franklin Roosevelt had written during World War II. He took for granted that any prayer composed by a political leader would necessarily be hypocritical. When his young Jewish friend insisted this was not the case, Solzhenitsyn was so surprised that he could not answer.

Carter says he prays often. Prayer like religion needs to be thought about carefully, although it need not be denied as a normal and even necessary part of life. Carter refuses to suppress his religious feelings fully or to secularize his faith. He has explained: "I'm not unique. There are a lot of people in this country who have the same religious faith. It is not a mysterious or mystical or magical thing."[12] He anticipates that persons who are unaware of the presence of God will have a quizzical attitude toward his religion. Carter maintains that his own faith has "always been something I've discussed very frankly throughout my adult life."

Coming down from New York, Mailer visited the Plains Baptist Church and attended the Sunday Bible class for men which is conducted once a month (in his turn) by Jimmy Carter. Mailer especially found the church architecture satisfying. The building is painted white and has a ceiling of gracious wooden eaves. Two "splendid old chairs with red velvet seats" stand on either side of the pulpit. An elegant church for such a small town, Mailer concluded, and he hoped that its architect was the town carpenter. Mailer speculated that whoever he was, he must have dwelt with ease in the proportions and needs of ecclesiastical space in his own lifetime. The congregation sang along with the choir, "the words full of Christian exaltation, their sword of love quivering in the air, that secret in the strength of Christianity where the steel is smelted from tears." He remembered the hymn, "I will sing the wondrous story of the Christ who died for me." During another hymn, Mailer is not sure exactly which, one of the choir members took out his harmonica and played "with feeling pure enough to take one back to the last campfires of a Confederate Army." To the visitor, he seemed to stir "old river reeds out of the tendrils of the past."

One of Carter's former pastors emphasizes he is not the Messiah. The American people should not expect the president to be a new Moses who will lead them into the promised Land, or even a prophet like Elijah. He points out that Carter has never represented religion as a panacea which will solve all problems. Unfortunately, religious claims do not mean that a man's character is above reproach or that he is necessarily honest. The cynicism which remains about earlier public piety comes from hard experience. But religion can be an important clue to the depths of a leader's personality and experience. Carter's character is inexplicable apart from his new birth. Whether it will make him a better and more effective president remains to be seen. However, his religious beliefs are important psychologically and politically. Critics need to understand what they are before debating them. Carter's convictions have intruded into public life; they are phenomena to be examined. How is one to establish empathy with them?

RELIGION IN THE ELECTION CAMPAIGN

Carter, among the candidates, seemed different from the beginning. An early campaign rally in the South began with a musical warm-up. If a country music group was present, the musicians would play the soulful "Dixie," the martial "Battle Hymn of the Republic," and the joyful "This Is My Country." Carter received the usual acclaim when he appeared at the podium. As the roar of applause subsided, he spoke almost without inflection, often in single words and phrases. The emotional pitch engendered by the music continued to rise, but in an unusual way. Carter's strange monotone was almost hypnotic. He used no text or cards and no stock jokes. Quiet was seldom broken by applause. At times, breaking off his speech in mid-phrase without any real end, he would ask for questions.

John R. Coyne, Jr., a former presidential speech writer, observes that a typical Carter address often has a double character.[13] One part touches what is called the problem, the so-called issues of the campaign. It is interspersed or followed by a second part filled with words that have emotive meaning for his audience: *truth, decency, forgiveness,* and *love.* "Filled with love," was a phrase Carter used often on the stump. Coyne points out that certain code words strung together express a spiritual framework, indeed a whole system of values which Carter shares with his audience. Whereas other candidates often do not speak within a consistent moral framework, Carter presents a context in which issues can be resolved. Coyne concludes, "And that context is nothing less than the Christian religion. . . . It's not possible to understand Carter's politics without his religion."[14]

Carter comes through as more than a personality. The audience recognizes a man of character who has depths that lie beneath the surface. As a political orator, Carter is effective because his sincerity is felt by the audience. Reeves, whom we cited earlier, wrote in May, 1976, that "the yearning crowds seem to come away believing, including a surprisingly high proportion of the working press. We want to believe, too."[15]

Carter speaks about values, faith in God, morality. "The American people are good . . . decent . . . honest . . . open." The press does not get the usual stock answers it so often expects. Carter is not easily dismissed just as a conservative or a liberal. To be sure, other candidates charged that he is evasive, waddles, and waffles. But to the majority of his audience, he speaks of reality. Coyne argues that as a devout Christian, Carter will know better than to attempt to build a perfect society here on earth. Instead, he will try to improve the present one. "And an essentially Christian plan for improvement might not hurt a bit. I do know we could do worse. We have. Consistently."[16]

CARTER'S LANGUAGE

It is important to recognize that Carter comes from a part of the country where Christian theism has not been challenged by skepticism as much as elsewhere; an inclusive Christian common sense continues. The University of Chicago Church Historian, Martin Marty, has commented on Carter's "Jesusity." It is cultural, he says. "For Jimmy Carter to say he is 'born again' is like you or I saying 'good morning.' There is no threat in those words."[17] Christianity is still accepted as the community ideology in the South in a more pervasive way than in the North. Garry Wills remarks, "But he could not avoid Jesus talk, even if he wanted to, where he comes from."[18] Every turn of a radio dial brings a hymn or a sermon. "Jesus talk is, at the least, a kind of static in the air. . . . It is a stikum or social glue.''

Carter thinks in the Christian terms which are native to his background—sin, forgiveness, and salvation. Such language is not just rational but emotive, dominating in the crises of birth, death, and middle age, and giving ultimate direction. As Nietzsche acknowledged, when such a heritage is destroyed, chaos or nihilism may set in.[19] This phenomenon is explicable in sociological terms, but not necessarily in its entirety. Religion provides inclusive meanings and perspectives. Robert Coles comments: ''As for his religious beliefs, so much mentioned and analyzed these days, he is less edgy when they come up for discussion.''[20] *In Why Not the Best?,* Carter speaks of such greats as Reinhold Niebuhr, Paul Tillich, and at one point Sören Kierkegaard, the Danish founder of existentialism who lived in the last century. Coles is emphatic, however, that Carter is not a religious or theological name-dropper.

Carter's faith is ''strong and of long duration,'' says Coles. It is what George Eliot would have called ''ardent.'' Carter is not one who has suddenly or abruptly turned to God because of psychiatric turmoil, family trouble, or for some social or political purpose. Throughout his lifetime, he has attempted to be a loyal, practicing member of his own religious community, professing faith in Christ's redemptive promise.

Coles insists Carter is neither self-righteous nor complacent when he confesses his beliefs and his ''condition'' before God. His tough political instincts do not reflect a lack of faith or serious psychological inconsistency. Carter simply tries to be a believing Christian, a human being living in a world of men and not of angels. He can be quite subtle and thoughtful, speaking theologically, expressing a kind of Christian existentialism. ''He sees himself as no great exception, religiously speaking.''[21] He believes that millions of Americans think and feel about the Bible and God as he does. They try to integrate their thoughts and feelings, as he does, into lives that are inevitably flawed, sinful, materialistic, but not "impulsive, bizarre, irregular, or crazy."

FEAR OF DEATH

A perennial theme of religion is death and dying. Carter was asked how he deals with the possibility of assassination in his own mind. He replied, "Well, in the first place, I'm not afraid of death."[22] Asked why not, he replied: "It's part of my religious belief. I just look at death as not a threat. It's inevitable, and I have an assurance of eternal life." Carter said that there is no feeling on his part that he has to live, or that he is immune to danger. The termination of his physical life is relatively insignificant in his concept of over-all existence. He added that he does not say this in any mysterious way. He just does not worry about his life.

FAITH AND DOUBT SET PERIMETERS

Carter was asked about his lack of doubts in an interview with Bill Moyers and replied:

> I obviously don't know all the answers to philosophical questions and theological questions—the kind of questions that are contrived. But the things that I haven't been able to answer, in theory or supposition, I just accept them and go on—things that I can't influence or change.
>
> But doubts about my faith? No.
>
> Doubt about my purpose of life? I don't have any doubts about that.[23]

What are the historical roots of Carter's faith?

THREE STRANDS OF CARTER'S RELIGION

E. Brooks Holifield, Professor of American Church History at Emory University in Atlanta, Georgia, believes that Carter's faith is a mixture of at least three historical traditions. One tradition comes from a form of Southern evangelicalism which has roots in the Puritan era. A second reflects the conviction of a religious pluralism which was accepted in late eighteenth-century America. A third tradition is indebted to more recent and sophisticated Christian political realism. Holifield remarks, "The compound may at first seem incongruous and it is the source of confusion among those now trying to understand the Carter phenomenon."[24] Holifield points out that the Southern Baptist Convention remains one of the last great repositories of the Puritan tradition in America. Like the later Puritans, it honors a set of inward religious experiences which it believes to be necessary for true church membership. These are developed as "conversion," "regeneration," or "rebirth."

Such experiences are not understood as a new revelation from God. God's will is already made known in the Bible. Instead, the new birth brings responsibilities for personal growth and control over such passions as anger, lust, pride, and fear. It is an experience of forgiveness, an undeserved gift, deeply felt and understood in highly personal terms as a "relationship to Christ." Nor is it mystical absorption into the divine. Conversion elicits the positive virtues of love and compassion. Carter describes his own experience of forgiveness and salvation as one that issues in strenuous discipline, inner commitment, and introspective watchfulness. He identified it for an appreciative United Methodist Conference in Atlanta in 1972, as "a continuing search in my own heart for a corrective attitude toward my natural inclinations."

27

Unlike the early American Puritans, Carter accepts the tradition of separation of church and state. Holifield describes the history of this doctrine as an alliance of opposites. Jefferson's Enlightenment party feared the tyranny of the churches and their leaders. Dissenting religious groups believed that government support corrupted the religious community. The two, disparate as they were, worked together against the religious establishment. Jefferson's contemporary, the Baptist John Leland, supported his efforts to secure religious freedom in Virginia. Faithful to this tradition, Carter scrupulously distinguished between his churchmanship and his political office while governor. He abolished the ostentatious Sunday services that Lester Maddox had established in the governor's mansion. Carter further advised members of his local church that they visit him as personal guests only.

The third strain in Carter's thought, political realism, has its background in his reading of the works of Reinhold Niebuhr. The evangelical tradition did not provide detailed categories for dealing with many complicated issues. Carter came to appreciate what Niebuhr was saying as the responsibilities of power came upon him. His reading of Niebuhr began in the 1960s. His friend, William Günter, now an associate justice of the Georgia Supreme Court, gave Carter a copy of a compilation of lengthy excerpts from Niebuhr's writings entitled *Reinhold Niebuhr on Politics*.[25] The two men began having periodic informal discussions about theology. Niebuhr's writings, in Günter's words, became "a political Bible" for Carter. The two politically involved Christians agreed that "love and kindness meant a great deal in one-to-one relationships but not as much in dealings with structures and corporate groups." Carter has often quoted Niebuhr's belief: "The sad duty of politics is to establish justice in a sinful world." Niebuhr's influence was obvious in the Governor's address given on Law Day at the University of Georgia. Carter argued that the fallibility of man and the conventions of society always prevent us from "achieving perfection." Yet more positively, he added that Martin Luther King, Jr., symbolized the continuing effort to achieve justice in an imperfect society.

A ROMAN CATHOLIC COMMENT

Is the president too pious? An editorial in the Jesuit edited magazine *America* commented: "It is not the social element in Jimmy Carter's religion that unnerves secularists but the personal one."[26] Most American politicians, the editorial explained, are at least nominally members of some church. But they are not expected to have what medieval theologians call *pietas,* that is, a firm sense of a loving and filial union with God. Carter's phrase is the conviction of "an intimate personal relationship with God."

But, *America* argues, piety as thus understood should be found in everyone who takes religion seriously. It cites the work of the French Jesuit theologian, Léonace de Grandmaison. In his *Personal Religion,* written more than fifty years ago, de Grandmaison commented: "Personal religion, piety, although . . . not the whole of true religion, is nevertheless the center and heart of it." The principal function of the social element of religion is the inspiration, maintenance, and direction of piety. The present American concern about religion is not as new or dramatic as some critics have suggested. Actually, Carter is closer to the roots of the national heritage than his critics have allowed.

In its editorial, *America* noted that different Christian communions fulfill their function in somewhat similar ways. Among Christians, piety is inspired primarily by a devotion toward Jesus; it has a general direction toward service. The Roman Catholic editor finds perfectly intelli-

29

gible the comment Carter made in June, 1976, at the convention of the Disciples of Christ in Lafayette, Indiana: "God has work for each one of us as individuals and wants us to demonstrate as best we can the life of Christ."

THE PROBLEM OF EVIL

Carter's approach is a practical one, as evidenced in the following incident. A visitor took the liberty of calling Carter's attention to the dichotomy between the fundamental simplicities of a good moral life as they appear in the Epistle of James, the book studied in his Bible class, and the "insuperable complexities of moral examination opened by Kierkegaard," whom Carter cites.[27] From his reading of the Danish father of existentialism, the visitor concluded that we cannot know the moral role we have. He cited a statement made by Carter in an interview with Bill Moyers, in which Carter had commented he felt he might be doing God's will when he had a sense of peace and self-assurance. Had Carter considered that God might be in anguish at what he had failed to accomplish? The visitor cited the Hasidic tale of Rabbi Zusya. The Rabbi begged God to reveal himself to him. When God did so, Zusya crawled under the bed and howled in fear like a dog. He called out, "O God, please do not reveal yourself to me." Did Carter not have any realization that God is close to losing? Christ believed that he would succeed, but died on a cross and failed. Carter replied soberly and thoughtfully that he did not spend as much time as people might expect exploring the depths of such questions. Maybe he ought to be more concerned. But he did not think his personal beliefs were to be enacted by government.

Carter's Baptist faith, like Kierkegaard's Lutheran Christianity, recognizes that the basic human problem is one of alienation. According to Christianity, the deepest roots of alienation are religious and not just economic. Ultimately, alienation can be overcome only by the grace of God. At this point, Christianity brings practical results in character, enabling man to conquer fear and guilt. This has been Carter's experience. He is not perennially in conflict and turmoil. He claims to know salvation and finds self-assurance through faith in a reality greater than himself. Christian faith and the democratic revolution are for him deeply held life presuppositions. Morality, peace, and justice are not just empty slogans, but God's will.

CRITICISM

Carter has his critics. A variety of charges have been made in Coyne's "Niceguyin' His Way to the White House?" in the May 14, 1976, *National Review;* Steven Brill's "Jimmy Carter's Pathetic Lies," in *Harper's,* the same month, and James T. Wooten's, "The Well-Planned Enigma of Jimmy Carter," in the June 6, *New York Times.* Bill Moyers, commenting on the Democratic National Convention that nominated Carter, said: "I have never seen such a combination of religion, politics, and manipulative techniques."[28] He described Carter as a "soft-spoken Georgia swain wearing a brick in a velvet glove."[29] What the delegates at the convention wanted, according to Moyers, was a priest and not a politician. Charles Henderson, formerly Chaplain of Princeton University, had observed earlier, "I believe that Jimmy Carter is now the Democratic front runner because he has read the signs of the times with greater sensitivity than have the other candidates."[30] Henderson believes that Carter reinforces the strong popular demand that government perform a distinctly sacral function.

The Religion of President Carter

Should the president assume the role of a religious leader? Henderson argues this is what Carter has done. He charges that Carter has a habit of slurring the distinction between the sacred and the secular. Carter has implied that the nation's social and spiritual problems come from the same cause and are amenable to the same solutions. Henderson says it is a "sentimental illusion to believe that complex political problems can be solved by an appeal to 'compassion and love.' "[31] Clare Booth Luce notes that the fusing of Christian doctrine with political power in the name of morality and social justice is not new. But she believes a religious leader should be a religious leader and a political leader should be a political leader. "Whoever has attempted to combine these roles has, throughout history, failed badly at one or the other, and usually both."[32]

Walter Dean Burnham of MIT predicted Carter's rise much earlier than other political scientists. He does not explain it on any simply religious grounds, but from the claim that activist liberalism as a national political force is now in receivership. Carter has had appeal in a situation in which both activist liberalism and the more conservative combatants of 1968 and 1972, are exhausted. He offers hope at a time that the American political system seems gripped by a "pervasive and intractable crisis." Politically, Carter has a vision of the realities of electoral politics which has transcended both sides. More than this, he has been able to construct a paradigm and an organization to implement it. This is reinforced by Carter's recognition of the religious overtones of the presidency. Asked by a local Baptist minister why he was not serving the church rather than engaging in the dubious business of politics, Carter compared his state senate district to "a church with 80,000 members."

Burnham emphasizes, "Jimmy Carter has orchestrated an appeal that is brilliantly adapted to the volatile politics of 1976."[33] He points to Carter's theme, "Government should be as good as the American people.'' He argues that the key to Carter's success is his ''wholehearted embrace of Middle America's attitudes and ambiguities.'' He emphasizes that Carter's ''*bona fides* are established through his obvious commitment to evangelical Protestant religion in his personal life.'' To his audience, Carter is profoundly optimistic and reassuring. His critics should not overlook the fact that he has offered an integrative, healing leadership to an electorate not willing to be told that its moral judgments are inadequate.

DANGERS

Of course, there are dangers in any religiously grounded hope. Carter reaffirms the American dream and sense of mission in the backlash of Watergate. The best days of the nation are yet ahead, in the future, he proclaims. But can the ultimate assurance of religion control even short-term trends? And who knows what the longer course of history will be? Carter shows confidence in the face of crisis. But can a new and evidently religious president really change anything in world affairs or even in domestic politics? Perhaps it is not just cynics alone but realists who are entitled to be pessimists. Carter says he will use atomic and hydrogen weapons only for defense of the nation. Suppose this becomes necessary. What will be the end of his affirmations of love and brotherhood amid atomic cinders? A recent public opinion survey showed that ninety-four percent of the citizens of the United States believe in God. Nearly seventy percent are convinced that there is life after death. Political capital sometimes has been made of such beliefs in earlier administrations. Religion can be used to cover up reluctance to deal with concrete problems and circumstances.

LOVE AND JUSTICE

Three days after his nomination for president at the New York Democratic Convention, Jimmy Carter taught his Sunday School class in Plains, Georgia. He has served in this capacity in the small community for nearly two decades. The Sunday School lesson concerned salvation through faith in Jesus Christ and the Savior's vicarious death for sinners—a cardinal Christian doctrine. The teacher spoke from sound Baptist scriptural grounds when he said a person must confess that he is sinful before he can be saved. Then Carter asked what Christian love means practically. "Obedience," came an answer. "No," replied Carter. "Simple justice." Carter's answer clarified his outlook at a crucial point. Love is expressed at least in justice. Carter's religion is not intended as an escape from reality.

For Carter love means care, becoming personally involved. The enemy of love is not as much power or justice as cynicism and the inability to care deeply. In God's sight, persons are not just an "It" but a "Thou." Carter seeks to enter into personal communion with them because God has entered into communion with him in Jesus. He often quotes a phrase that he learned from a Cuban minister, Eloy Cruz, whom he accompanied on an evangelistic mission to New England Puerto Ricans in 1967: "Our Saviour has hands which are very gentle, and he cannot do much with a man who is hard."[34]

Whatever else Carter is, he must be classified as a moralist. He remains serious about ethics and good and evil. For Carter's conviction, right and wrong are not relative. Carter's sense of discipline takes its cue from Jesus' parable of the talents. Part of his sense of responsibility belongs to the life of the farmer as he plants crops, tills the soil, and waits patiently for the harvest. One cannot reap unless he sows. Carter's election was the result of careful planning and hard work. One cannot simply seize the day and succeed. Irresponsibility leads to failure. At its best, Carter's religion makes clear the tension between what is and what ought to be. He claims to seek to do God's will because it is right, not because it is expedient. At the same time, he expresses a sense of unworthiness and sin. Perfectionism is denied, but effort is called for in response to duty.

It is in these terms that a populist Christian critique has come out of Plains, Georgia: technology and political power can corrupt. Property and prosperity may make both men and nations insensitive to human need. America is rich and prosperous, but there is crime in the streets. Its cities too often seem to be decaying from within. Carter seems to have tried to spell out his message in terms of the symbolism of the town of Plains itself. Mailer describes it as offering ''an unmistakable well-ordered patina, a promise that the mysterious gentility of American life'' is present. Carter believes the morality of leaders and the models they hold before the people are of first importance. Of course, all abuse cannot be dissipated at once by good intentions. Institutional strategies are necessary. But we must also achieve motivation for reform. The president's Christian idealism explains a significant part of his character and is linked to his ambition.

2. A Southern Baptist Christian

IDENTIFYING SOUTHERN BAPTISTS

A president's religion can be classified in a variety of ways. To which church or confession did he belong? Was he faithful or unfaithful in his duties toward it? Was his relation simply a formal one or more deeply motivated? Carter has been a responsible and active Christian layman in his own denomination. Duke K. McCall, president of Southern Baptist Seminary at Louisville, Kentucky, has commented: "The trouble is that Jimmy Carter not only is a Southern Baptist—he talks like one."[1] President McCall complains:

> News reporters have ventilated a lot of half-baked tripe in their columns and on the air. Some of them, including national television news commentators, are plain incompetent, not because they did not know about Southern Baptists before Jimmy Carter broke on the scene, but because they did not bother to do adequate research. . . . Southern Baptists have many responsible leaders in business and civic life, as well as political life, but they have not yet been seen as typically Baptists.

McCall concedes:

> Southern Baptists really are different. We cannot make ourselves look like the main line church bodies in America. On the spectrum of religious bodies in the United States, we are right-wing, evangelical (we would say evangelistic). We have a more puritan ethic in our official pronouncements, if not in our personal practices, than many other religious bodies. . . . Paint us purple with passion if a public official advocates any form of gambling. Color us absent in the ecumenical meetings. Paint us red with rage if one of our leaders takes a stand on a public issue with which individually we do not agree. . . . So God forgive us. We act just like human beings while claiming to be the children of God.[2]

Baptist roots are not only in the Protestant revolt, but in that movement which historians call "the Second Wave of the Reformation."[3] Lutherans, Calvinists, and Anglicans established inclusive state churches. Baptists belonged to the disestablished sectarian movement which was often persecuted. Southern Baptists also share in the heritage of the American Revolution and the War Between the States. Now worldwide in membership, Baptists initially were a small voluntary Christian body, socially unaccepted and without tolerance by the state. Anabaptists were notorious as rebaptizers.

THE FREE CHURCHES

The mainstream of the Reformation, with church-state ties, practiced the baptism of infants shortly after their birth. The more sober Anabaptists believed that the New Testament taught that baptism was to be restricted to those old enough to understand personally and accept the Christian faith. Since infants are passive and have no personal accountability, infant baptism violated the idea of believer's baptism and the regenerate church. At a later time, in early seventeenth-century England, immersion was insisted upon as the proper mode of baptism to express a personal death to a self-centered life and a resurrection to a Christ-centered life.

The early Baptists of England believed they were following the New Testament model. Since each member is theoretically a committed Christian, each church can govern itself and does not need hierarchical control. Voluntary support of the congregation eliminates state support and control. Obviously, in a time when the churches were state controlled, such a religious movement would be small, misunderstood, and even persecuted.

For more than two hundred years, the Baptist movement was persecuted by the major Christian bodies including both Roman Catholics and Protestants. Voluntary "gathered" churches, like the Baptists, attempted to reverse a millenium and a half of church history in their advocacy of the separation of church and state. Following the Protestant Reformation, a combination of political rulers and church officials successfully suppressed this "witness." On the Continent, Holland gave the Baptists a place of refuge. In the seventeenth century, they eventually won some freedom of worship in England. In the United States, with religious freedom guaranteed, they flourished on the frontier. Today they constitute the majority religion in large sections of the South and Southwest.

BEGINNINGS IN AMERICA

The initial Baptist Church in North America was established by Roger Williams at Providence, Rhode Island, in 1639, after he protested the church-state union practiced in the Massachusetts Bay Colony.[4] The first organized Baptist association embraced a group of five churches in Philadelphia in 1707. After the American Revolution, a national body was established in the same city in 1814. It was known as the General Missionary Convention of the Baptist Denomination in the United States for Foreign Missions, and it met in session every three years. Differences over slavery, centralized publication, and denominational control led to the organization of the Southern Baptist Convention at Augusta, Georgia, in 1845.

Together, North and South, white and black, Baptists are the largest Protestant group in the United States, second in membership only to Roman Catholics. Approximately a quarter of the church members in the United States are Baptists. At the beginning of the Second World War, the Southern Baptist Convention operated in nineteen states, primarily in the South and border areas. Today its membership is nationwide and embraces approximately forty-three percent of the total Baptist population. Its constituency is largely white by race, although an increasing number of Spanish-Americans, blacks, and other ethnic groups are joining its congregations. In total there are some one hundred thousand Baptist churches in the country with a combined membership of about thirty million. Of the twenty-nine Baptist groups or associations, some are small in size. Since Baptist polity gives local autonomy for each church, there are individual churches which are fully independent. The largest groups of Baptists outside the Southern Baptist Convention are made up of blacks.

Baptists seek to base their confessions of faith on the New Testament. A summary of their ideals issued in the United States in 1964 exemplifies their outlook. It proclaims the ultimate authority is Jesus Christ, although the practical authority is the Bible. Inclusively, the church is the fellowship of persons who profess a personal faith in

Jesus Christ as the Messiah and rightful religious authority. At the local level, each church is a voluntary community of baptized believers, seeking to conduct its programs under the leadership of Christ. Salvation is a gift of God in Jesus Christ, conditioned only on trust in Him and its acceptance. Baptism and the Lord's Supper are primarily seen as ordinances to express prior faith and commitment and to show forth the Christian faith. Baptists emphasize that the Bible, properly interpreted, is God's inspired revelation for faith and practice. Although extensive religious education programs are conducted, each individual ultimately has freedom to make decisions. The new relationship with Christ results in a sense of stewardship of life, money, and talents.

FREEDOM OF CONSCIENCE

Morris B. Abram, a distinguished Jewish leader and personal friend of Carter, tells of a conversation he had at a meeting with intellectuals during the election in the Washington, D.C., area.[5] He had spoken in support of Carter's candidacy. At the close of the session, he was asked by a man "breathing fire": "Did you read what Carter is quoted as having said in the *New York Times* about conscientious objection?" "Yes," Abram answered. "And I agree." Carter had said it was all right to violate the law if the law goes against God's command, provided you are willing to pay the penalty. Abram asked, "What's wrong with that? It was Martin Luther King's position and it's my own." The interrogator called attention to the fact that Carter had spoken of God's command. "What if God told him to do some irrational, disastrous act?"

Abram attempted to explain that to a Southern Baptist, conscience speaks for God. Jimmy Carter is a rational man and does not claim communication with voices. Abram

41

tried to translate. He said Carter was only expressing Jefferson's position. To be sure, Jefferson would have used other language and spoken of the supremacy of the natural law and "the commands of nature and nature's God." Carter's defender noted that Southern Catholics and Jews as well as other Protestants are not the least put off by the Southern Baptist way of communicating religious beliefs. Dramatic expressiveness and hyperbole are recognized as part of religious exhortation. The Southern Baptists' depth of faith is not questioned. Fellow citizens have learned to sprinkle salt on the adjectives and metaphysics!

BIBLE-BELT RELIGION

Earlier in the century, H. L. Menken, writing in the *American Mercury,* applied the term "Bible-belt religion" to rural sections of the South where piety is expressed by earnest praying, hymn singing, Bible study, and proselyting.[6] The Bible-belt *ethos,* still living today, has century-old roots. The people who lived in the South on the frontier in the eighteenth century were close to nature in the rough. A host of forces and obstacles had to be combated in their environment. Their reaction was often emotional more than intellectual. Informal worship services suited their temperament and need for excitement.

The frontier was far removed from the Enlightenment rationalism of the Eastern seaboard. The popular attitude was expressed by a Kentucky Baptist.[7] He observed that Voltaire, disgusted with the corruptions and oppressions of the religion of his own country, set out to destroy "the religion of Christ" in the whole world. Mistakenly, he proclaimed the innate goodness of man as against original sin. The deist, Tom Paine, who fought in the American revolution, is cited even more often. James Gallaher in *The*

Western Sketch-Book recounted: "Tom Paine scoffed at all that was sacred in religion, profanely mocked and blasphemed the ordinances of God. O, it was a tremendous eruption of the bottomless pit. The shock had well nigh thrown down the hope of the church."[8] But the popular song ran:

> The *world,* the Devil and Tom Paine, Have try'd their force, but all in vain.
> They can't prevail, the reason is, The Lord defends the Methodist.[9]

In antebellum days, before the War Between the States, the Southern clergy were the foundation of social coherence. After the defeat of the South in 1865, the societal obligation to belong to the church became a general one; the whole population had to perform the function which earlier belonged to the clergy. Southern whites at times found relief by subscribing to the tenets of a guilt-oriented theology. The singing of "The Old Rugged Cross" was joined to the reaffirmation of accepted values: If God be for us, who can be against us? Religion, as so often, was aculturated. There has been a sense of regional apartness and superiority with pride in specific convictions about the role of women, emphasis on personal extroversion, pride in small-town manners, in an Anglo-Saxon heritage, distinctive speech accents, regional foods, and culinary styles. All bespeak regional apartness. Citizens of the American Middle West have not felt the need to construct such a defense.

THE SOUTHERN MYSTIQUE

Dwight Dorough comments that there is a *sine qua non* for the South. It is a thing of the mind. A particular character and point of view marks a Southerner. Maybe ''even in the South [it] is disappearing; but only in the South now does it move even thinly over the land and in those men who once knew the land.''[10]

To be sure, there is a wide variety, and stereotypes need to be avoided. Yet the legacy of the self-reliant individualism, love of land, together with strong family ties does apply to Carter. Religion in the South has been very personal. There has been a close affinity of politics and religion in a region preoccupied with emotionalism and moralism. Walter Hines Page writes of the pioneer preachers: ''Such men were cast in a large mold. They almost ranked themselves with the giants. They dealt directly with the fundamental emotions of men and with some of the great facts of the spiritual life.''[11] Page concludes that it was more impressive to have known one of these men than all the political and military heroes that have been since bred. Politicians may have been the greatest popular heroes, but preachers had the greater influence. This kind of practical Christianity has long been dominant in much of the South. The crisis ethos of evangelical Protestantism has been an attractive option to the average Southern churchman as he has seemed to have a continual rendezvous with destiny, confronting it existentially each day.

Carter's religiously grounded moralism belongs to this setting. The Baptist plain and simple meeting house tradition emphasizes honesty, good faith, and dependability. Critics have described the *ethos* negatively as over-moralized and puritanical in a bad sense. But such a charge can be made against any serious moralism. Celibacy is not advocated, but instead there is support for the family where love belongs to spouse and children. Typical of his background, Carter speaks out for the family even in the midst of an election campaign. It has even been suggested that he knows only bourgeois, middle class morality. Baptists were long known as people who oppose dancing, card playing, and drinking. The small sins have been at times a real preoccupation.

For Southern piety, God is understood as possessing heroic existence. His authority and disclosure of truth have about them realities of exactitude and finality, realness and concretion. The Southern cultural system makes metaphysical claims and imposes moral constraints. The Lord of heaven and earth is a requiring and demanding being, characteristically and predominately moral. Man's own nature cannot be perceived aright apart from what he expects. As the Father is, so must His children be. Man's life can be and is meant to be on a higher plane. Goodness is a quality which is not easily or automatically achieved. It is not identical with the ordinary consensus about what is valuable.

Living with the legacy of defeat in the War Between the States, the South does not share all of the optimism about man expressed in the North. Southern preaching emphasizes Christ's atoning death and the assurance of salvation, themes such as sin, crucifixion, and redemption. The central claim of Southern Christianity is explicit in Jesus' words, accepted by Carter, "Ye must be born again." Characteristically, the individual is expected to declare the "time when and the place where" his new birth began. Salvation gives knowledge that the Christian has passed from one state of existence, lostness, and condemnation by God, to a new state where guilt is pardoned and heaven is assured. Christians are called to be disciples in both status and behavior. They are expected to make an intense appraisal of the values and practices of their lives, purging the dross and building up the soul.

CARTER'S CAREER AS A BAPTIST

One of the denominational leaders who sent Carter out on his first missionary crusades into the North has remarked that his religion is not something that can be codified and put in a drawer separate from the rest of his life. He does not have to evince piety to show that he is a good person. There is no theater. He is constrained but does not need to strain to be a Christian. Christianity means for Carter adult responsibility, a sense of sin, destiny, and redemptive power. His concerns are practical, and he is not interested in theological hairsplitting. For him, the question is not how high you jump but how straight you walk, the denominational official concluded.

Politically, Carter believes in responsible participation in government by persons with religious convictions. His own position is more in the tradition of Sen. Mark Hatfield of Oregon, who has remained in the Senate, than that of Harold Hughes of Iowa, who felt he must withdraw from the Senate to continue his Christian life. Carter believes that positive results can be achieved, although he is not utopian. His Christian faith gives him a conviction that politics can be a full-time vocation in the world. Assuredly, he mixes ambition and devotion.

Carter's roots in Plains do not explain everything about his outlook. He has felt the impact of the nation and the world while still remaining in the South. Atlanta is a remarkably cosmopolitan city, an oasis in the Bible-belt. Carter belonged to a dynamic and open congregation while he was governor. More than scholasticism or biblicism dominated the church. Its minister fought for integration even as Carter ended racial discrimination in government. Carter participated in his denomination's "pioneer missions" to the North and West. Changes were effected in his life as well as with converts. Aculturation is not as strong in these areas as in the South. New ideas are accepted and can be tried out before they are used in the more settled or traditional parts of the church. What Carter learned seems to have carried over into his political career.

"Ye are the salt of the earth," said Jesus. "But that salt too often is kept by Christians in a cellophane bag," remarked Carter's former minister in Atlanta as he reflected homiletically on the New Testament text.[12] In an attempt to overcome ingrownness, his congregation undertook "Operation Touch." A missionary outreach in Honduras bespoke concern for what is sometimes called "the global village." At home, there was a project for the underprivileged in an impoverished part of Atlanta. The Carters not only contributed generously, Rosalynn put on her jeans and helped clean up the premises when the operation began. The same minister assigned Governor Carter responsibility for teaching a Sunday School class called the "Last Chance." It included a number of members whose interest in the church had diminished even as their means and prestige had increased. Some who had not attended worship services for a long time started to come again. Upon inquiry, the minister discovered Carter had fulfilled his duty to witness by sending them a personal note and reminding them of their responsibility.

CONFLICT WITH THE BAPTIST ESTABLISHMENT

While in Atlanta, Carter was open and growing in his denominational activities. An active member of the national Brotherhood Board, he attended meetings regularly. But he was not complacent or servile to the clergy! This fact is made clear from the following incident. While governor, Carter was once asked why there was so much lawlessness in certain parts of the state. He replied that one major cause was a failure to enforce the law evenhandedly. A bad model was set by prohibition laws. Carter advocated full citizenship, beginning at eighteen years of age. He argued that a man who could vote and was expected to defend his country, should also be able to buy an alcoholic drink. Almost at once, the newspapers reported that Carter favored repeal; this was true, at least in the context in which he had spoken.[13]

Alarmed and offended, the leaders of the Georgia Baptist Convention, meeting in its annual session in the fall of 1973, passed a resolution against the governor's position. When the resolution was made public in the press, Carter dispatched a personal letter to the Convention. He knew Baptists have wide influence and political importance as the largest religious body in the state. Carter wished and expected his letter to be read publicly before adjournment. Convention leaders, declaring the last session a worship service, did not present the letter. Instead, they sent a delegation to meet with the governor. Carter is reported to have spoken forthrightly, indeed in anger, when the delegation finally came to call on him. He, too, had a theological library, he told them. He did not agree with their allegation that liquor is the number one national problem. There are others—poverty, injustice, and discrimination.

PERSONAL INTERVIEW WITH BILL MOYERS

Carter's present state of faith may be appraised at least in part from his interview with Bill D. Moyers, a Southern Baptist minister.[14] Carter explained that the fact that a person has deep religious convictions does not necessarily mean that he thinks he's always right or that God has ordained him for a dominant position. "Although I have prayed a good bit—and do—I've never asked God to let me be president." "What do you pray for then?" Moyers asked.

Carter replied, "Well, I ask God to let me do what's right, and let me do what's best, that my life may be meaningful in an optimum way.'' Carter does not claim to be better than anyone else. ''I recognize my own shortcomings·and sinfulness and my need to improve, and the need for forgiveness from the people around me and from God.'' Carter remarked that when Jesus was asked about the great commandments from God which should direct our life, he said to love God with all your heart and soul and mind, and love your neighbor as yourself. Carter explained he tries to take that summary of Christian theology and let it be something through which he searches for meaningful existence. For him, every day is meaningful.

Carter called attention to Paul Tillich's comment that religion is a search for a relationship between us and God and us and our fellow human beings. When we quit searching, in effect, we've lost our relation. When we become self-satisfied, proud, sure, at that point we lose the self-searching, the humility, the subserviency to God's will, the intimate understanding of other people's needs, and the mere inclination to be accommodating, and in that instant, we lose our religion.

From his new birth, Carter has become able to look at the world in practical terms, to accept defeat, to get pleasure out of successes, to be at peace with the world. One of the things which came from his conversion experience was concern for people. For instance, he stood in a factory shift line early one morning at the General Electric plant in Erie, Pennsylvania, shaking hands with the employees.

''Everybody that comes through there, when I shake hands, for that instant, I really care about them in a genuine way. . . . I don't want to insinuate that I'm better than other people. I've still got a long way to go. . . .''

''But you care though?'' asked Moyers.

''I care.''

''You have found that you care about people.''

''I do.''

3. The Religion Of The Presidents

IS RELIGION AN INTRUSION?

Arthur M. Schlesinger, Jr. wrote at the end of April, 1976, in the *Wall Street Journal,* about what he called the "Carter phenomenon."[1] Chiding Carter for bringing religion into the campaign, he quoted Reinhold Niebuhr: "Religion is more frequently a source of confusion than of light in the political realm." Schlesinger emphasized that the word "God" does not appear in the Constitution. He wrote:

> This conviction of the frailty of man in face of the awful mystery of the Almighty is the essence of historic Christianity.

But Christianity is more than this, as Carter affirms. It has not only a doctrine of creation, but also of Incarnation. Schlesinger has reported only one aspect of its truth. Christian influence on American life has been more positive. What is Carter's relation to his predecessors' faith and the traditions of the presidency? Bliss Isley in his book, *The Presidents, Men of Faith,* appraises his theme positively:

The Religion of President Carter

> In comparison with other nations, the United States has been fortunate in its chief executives. The Bible, the church and their homes served them well.[2]

The mother of one president was a minister. Three presidents had fathers who were clergymen; five married parsonage-born women. One president had a regular charge; another served as a supply preacher. Two others doubled as chaplains when they were colonels in the army.

All American presidents since Washington have taken their oath of office on an open Bible. Of course, leaders have varied in the intensity of their religious conviction. The religion of the presidency has embraced a wide variety of Protestant denominations. John F. Kennedy has been the only Roman Catholic president. Separation of church and state precludes any simple uniformity. It is not the responsibility of the president to patronize a particular cult as the representative of the people. Such a role has often fallen on kings and emperors in history. By contrast in the United States, a president is forbidden to favor any particular denomination. All support of religion by the state is denied by the Constitution. Disestablishment does not preclude an active religious life on the part of the chief executive. But his beliefs about the ultimate meaning of life and death are a private matter. State officials are not to interfere in church affairs except when public order or common decency are threatened. In fact, separation of church and state has allowed religion to flourish more than in countries where there have been state churches. The American situation has meant that there is freedom *for* rather than freedom *from* religion.

THE ENLIGHTENMENT

Care must be taken not to blur historical distinctions in a description of the religion of the presidency.[3] Enlightenment rationalism joined with Protestant dissenter protest to effect the full separation of church and state in a new American kind of polity. Although the Pilgrims, mostly Calvinist Puritans, had come to the Western hemisphere in search of religious liberty, they did not allow full freedom of conscience. Freed from the establishment of the mother country, they built their own theocracy in New England. Roger Williams and Ann Hutchison, for example, were expelled from the Massachusetts Bay Colony because of their protests against establishment. By the eighteenth century, religious zeal had diminished and indifference had set in. It is estimated that not more than five percent of the population was churchgoing at the time of the American revolution. Enlightenment belief in nature's God, not just Christian orthodoxy, is reflected in the Declaration of Independence.

In the spirit of Enlightenment rationalism, Washington and Jefferson conceived of God on the analogy of the perfect watchmaker. Christian and Deist beliefs were joined in their world view. They believed that the universe is orderly and gives overwhelming evidence of creation by a divine intelligence. God need not always intervene in the world, for it has its own built-in moral balance. To their abiding credit, the leaders of the Enlightenment championed tolerance and freedom, often in the face of bigotry. Their doctrine of human nature was an optimistic one. Ignorance, not sin, is the chief folly of man. Evil requires no special divine intervention, in that human wisdom and conscience can supply all the remedy that is needed. A more

53

pessimistic doctrine of man was reflected in a mistrust of rulers. A president like John Adams took this view, especially after the evident excesses of the French Revolution. The constitutional division of powers between the executive, legislative, and judicial branches of government was indebted to the Puritan Calvinistic tradition.

SEPARATION OF CHURCH AND STATE

Carter affirms the separation of church and state. What are the historical roots? It was first accepted in the South during the era of the American Revolution. Virginia set the pattern for the rest of the nation. Leo Pfeffer in *Church, State and Freedom* writes that the change in that state from an establishment probably more severe and oppressive than any other in the country was very swift. The almost complete separation and freedom acheived in little more than a decade may properly be called revolutionary.[4]

Four of the first five presidents were from Virginia. The era from 1768 to 1774 was known in that state as the time of the Great Persecution. Baptists in particular were whipped, beaten, arrested, fined, and imprisoned, sometimes on bread and water. Persons who denied the Trinity could be put in prison for as long as three years. A Unitarian or freethinker might even be denied the custody of his own children. James Madison, who was later to be the fourth president of the Republic, wrote to a friend in 1774:

> That diabolical, hell-conceived principle of persecution rages among some. . . . This vexes me the worst of anything whatever. There are at this time in the adjacent county not less than five or six well-meaning men in close jail for publishing their religious sentiments, which in the main are very orthodox. I have neither patience to hear, talk, or think of

anything relative to this matter; for I have squabbled and scolded, abused and ridiculed, so long about it to little purpose, that I am without common patience. So I must beg you to pity me, and pray for liberty of conscience to all.[5]

THEORY

A variety of religious parties were tolerated in the colonies, in part because the English government had not insisted on the same kind of uniformity in suppressing dissent as had the Spanish crown. The reasons were not just idealistic but rather based on economic self-interest. As early as 1750, a request was made in London by the Lords of Trade to the President of the Council which read:

A free exercise of religion is so valuable a branch of true liberty and so essential to the enriching and improving of a Trading Nation, it should ever be held sacred in his Majesty's Colonies. . . .[6]

Of course, it is more difficult to engage in trade with persons whom one seeks to destroy because of their religious beliefs. Ideologically, the doctrine of the English philosopher, John Locke, was influential in the American solution of the church-state problem and subsequently on the role of religion in the presidency. In his *First Letter Concerning Toleration,* Locke wrote:

The care of souls cannot belong to the civil magistrate because his power consists only in outward force, but true and saving religion consists in the inward persuasion of the mind.[7]

A Bill of Rights was part of the first State Constitution in Virginia and declared, ''All men are equally entitled to the free exercise of religion according to the dictates of conscience.''[8] The Anglican establishment in Virginia was

55

well protected by law, and its proponents continued to advocate recognition of the Christian religion by the state—government subsidy for parishes, ministers, and church education. Did the Bill of Rights mean that such churches could no longer draw public support? The issue was disputed for nearly a decade. Jefferson's Bill for Establishing Religious Freedom had been introduced in 1779. Only in January, 1786, under Madison's sponsorship, was the measure finally adopted. Full separation of church and state was effected in Virginia, preceding that in Massachusetts by nearly half a century. The wisdom of such a polity came to be evident practically, and was not just an abstract formula.

PRESIDENT CARTER AND THE FOUNDING FATHERS

The attitude of the first president, George Washington, was summed up bluntly by John Bell when he said that Washington was "a total stranger to religious prejudices, which have so often excited Christians of one denomination to cut the throats of those of another."[9] Paul F. Boller, Jr. after making an objective and detailed study of Washington's religion, concluded: "In the fight against bigotry in America, George Washington played a role second to none." This is true both while Washington was Commander-in-Chief of the Continental Army and when he was president. The first president wished to create a climate in the new country in which every man could "sit in safety under his own vine and fig tree and there shall be none to make him afraid."[10] To this end, he used the immense prestige of his office to encourage mutual tolerance and good will among Protestants, Catholics, and Jews.

Washington, a lifelong member of the Episcopal Church, was a vestryman and church warden in the Parish of Truro for many years. The office was a social and political one, not just religious. Washington was convinced that organized religion is a necessary basis for morality and social order. This is clear from his letters which abound in references to God, Providence, heaven and divine favor, especially during his later years. Rather than referring to God directly, Washington spoke in typically eighteenth century fashion of the "Great Architect," "Director of Human Events," "Author of the Universe," and "Invisible Hand."[11]

In the American tradition, sovereignty rests with the people. Yet it is often implied or said explicitly that ultimate rule belongs to God. The slogan, "In God We Trust," for example, appears on coins. What difference can such words make? Why should the Founding Fathers have been concerned about whether sovereignty belongs to God? In fact, the phrase affirms a higher criterion from which the popular will can be judged. The people may be mistaken. Their disposition is not the final standard of right and wrong. As the first Roman Catholic president, John F. Kennedy, affirmed, "the rights of man come not from the generosity of the state, but from the hand of God."[12] He was not simply affirming the tradition of his own church when he used this phrase. The doctrine of the rights of man, affirmed explicitly in the fundamental documents of the American Revolution, gives the ultimate basis for openness and change in American democracy.

Four references to God are included in the Declaration of Independence. The most famous, "all men are endowed by their Creator with certain inalienable Rights," reflects a commonly accepted religious basis. The Declaration states the new nation's acceptance of a higher law which had earlier been affirmed in both classical natural law and biblical religion.

It is the commonly accepted premise of American political life which renders all forms of political absolutism illegitimate. Providing a transcendent goal for political process, it does not contradict the separation of church and state. On the contrary, it supports this doctrine.

THOMAS JEFFERSON

Jefferson, author of the Declaration of Independence, was a philosopher as well as active leader of the fight for religious liberty in Virginia which was waged even as Washington's armies were in battle. Without his influence, American polity could have been different. In his *Notes on Virginia,* Jefferson wrote:

> But our rulers can have no authority over such natural rights, only as we have submitted to them. The rights of conscience we never submitted, we could not submit. We are answerable for them to our God. . . . Reason and free inquiry are the only effectual agents against error. Give a loose to them, they will support the religion by bringing every false one to their tribunal, to the test of their investigation. They are the natural enemies of error, and of error only.[13]

As a man of the Enlightenment, Jefferson was put off by Orthodoxy, its dogmatism and the fact that it had persecuted so often. "Is uniformity attainable?" he asked.

> Millions of innocent men, women and children, since the introduction of Christianity have been burnt, tortured, fined, imprisoned; yet we have not advanced one inch towards uniformity. What has been the effect of coercion? To make one half the world fools, and the other half hypocrites. To support roguery and error all over the earth.[14]

Jefferson had a lack of appreciation for sin characteristic of the Enlightenment. He wrote that Jesus "preaches the efficacy of repentance toward forgiveness of sin: I require a counterpoise of good works to redeem it."[15] No doubt, faith without works is dead! Jesus' ethic of love, however, was honored by the third president.

His [Jesus] moral doctrines, relating to kindred and friends, were more pure and perfect than those of the most correct of the philosophers . . . and they went far beyond . . . in inculcating universal philanthropy, not only to kindred and friends, to neighbors and countrymen, but to all mankind, gathering all into one family, under the bonds of love, charity, peace, common wants, and common aids.[16]

CIVIL RELIGION

Although there was indebtedness to Christianity, the American Republic did not simply espouse the Christian religion. No president has failed to mention God in his inaugural oration. Providence is often invoked but the name of Jesus does not appear in any inaugural address. A cynical observer could argue that a semblance of piety is merely one of the unwritten qualifications for the office of president. Reference to deity would be seen, then, as a bit more traditional but not essentially different from the present-day requirement of a pleasing television personality. The sociologist, Robert Bellah, argues that such an evaluation risks misunderstanding the phenomena.[17]

Considering the separation of church and state, Bellah asks how a president is justified in using the word "God" at all. His answer is that the separation of church and state has not denied the political realm a religious dimension. Personal religious belief and worship are viewed as strictly private matters. At the same time, certain common ele-

59

ments of religious orientation are shared by the majority of Americans. "These have played a crucial role in the development of American institutions and still provide a religious dimension for the whole fabric of American life, including the political sphere."[18] Bellah describes this public dimension as an American civil religion—a set of symbols, beliefs, and rituals. It has a highly important role in the inauguration of a president, for example, giving religious legitimation to the highest political authority.

In the tradition of the American presidency, God is not understood as just a watchmaker who is absent from the world. On the contrary, He is conceived as actively interested in the history of the country. Analogies have been drawn with ancient Israel ever since the founding of the nation. For example, Jefferson in his second inaugural address exclaimed, "I shall need, too, the favor of that Being in whose hands we are, who led our fathers, as Israel of old, from their native land and planted them in a country flowing with all the necessities and comforts of life."[19]

In this symbolism, Europe stands for Egypt and the United States is seen as the Promised Land. Providence, it is affirmed, has led Americans to establish a new republic, repudiating old tyrannies, civil and ecclesiastical. It is to be a light to all nations. The claim is not intended as either sectarian or in any specific sense Christian. It is important to note that it was made at a time when society was overwhelmingly Protestant. The Founding Fathers' primary concern was not to spare the feelings of the very small non-Christian minority. The first leaders of the nation were only expressing what they believed to be appropriate in the circumstances. They offered no substitute for Christianity. An exceptionally wide sphere of personal piety and voluntary social action was reserved to the churches; at the same time religion was not given state support.

NINETEENTH CENTURY

Enlightenment rationalism had already begun to decline by the time of Jefferson's presidency as the excesses of the French Revolution became clear. The revolt against revealed religion was overcome in the new piety which came in from the frontier. However, President Carter stands more in a Populist than an Enlightenment tradition. He has been compared with the seventh president, Andrew Jackson.

The hero of the battle of New Orleans brought the spirit of the West to the capital. Like Jefferson, he was a Populist but of a very different sort.

Throughout the remainder of the nineteenth century, American interests turned inward and away from Europe. There was territory to be won, a continent to be conquered. The key movement on the frontier was the revival, more an American than a European phenomenon. It was often coupled with camp meetings and religious assemblies where settlers came together in their covered wagons, remaining for weeks. Preaching was fervent, and its goal was personal conversion. More often than not, frontiersmen were ''low churchmen'' who did not favor priesthood, special clerical office, or prayerbooks.

American democracy, overwhelmingly Protestant, found unity in the myths of new beginning and manifest destiny. The break with Europe was not to be just political but one of the spirit. The new nation would not repeat the mistakes of the old world. The hymn, ''My Country 'Tis of Thee,'' was written in a New England Protestant seminary. ''Our Father's God to Thee, author of liberty,'' was a common sentiment. In fact, the religion and the culture of the new nation did interact positively.

61

The office of the president was inspired by a national dream which transcended sectarian differences. Even the tragedy of the Civil War which divided the nation into North and South, moderating optimism, did not end the growth of religion; it continued throughout the nineteenth century. The situation was very different from France where church leaders opposed new democratic institutions. One need only consider the course of events on the continent of Europe to see how different things might have been. The French Revolution was anticlerical to the core and attempted to set up an anti-Christian civil religion.

ABRAHAM LINCOLN

Until the Civil War, American symbolism focused largely on the Exodus, the revolution from the old lands across the waters. The War Between the States raised the deepest questions of national meaning in the tragic intensity of fratricidal strife.

The new religious outlook which appeared in the national life was expressed by President Lincoln. Lincoln's bust stands in Carter's study in Plains. Lincoln was not a church member, although he did attend the Presbyterian Church in Springfield, Illinois, which his wife joined following the death of a son. Yet Lincoln had religious depth lacking in the men of the Enlightenment. He had known rural Baptist frontier revivals in his early youth. There may have been a short period in his life when he rejected all religion.

Elton Trueblood in his *Abraham Lincoln, Theologian of Anguish,* has identified an important and impressive religious strain in Lincoln's later writings.[20] He had appropriated the Christian criticism of life and it contributed profoundly to his understanding of the crisis of the Republic.

Lincoln introduced the new themes of death, sacrifice,

and rebirth in speaking of the national life. Often highlighting birth images, he gave a new center to American history. Bellah points out that his addresses have a Christian quality but are not sectarian. Their symbolism is Christian while still separate from the Christian Church. Lincoln had a genuine apprehension of universal and transcendent religious reality as seen in, or one could almost say as revealed through, the experience of the American people.

Reinhold Niebuhr argues: "Lincoln's religious convictions were superior in depth and purity to those, not only of the political leaders of his day, but of the religious leaders of the era."[21] They were not as corrupted by polemical use of the slavery issue as those of much of the clergy.

SUMMARY OF THE AMERICAN EXPERIENCE

The American tradition of separation of church and state belonged to Lincoln as well as the Founding Fathers. It has been espoused unqualifiedly by Carter. Why did it survive in the United States while an established Church reappeared in France, for example? The United States had no Robespierre or Napoleon. Official church leadership was less exclusive or entrenched than in France, and thus anticlericalism was not widespread. The basic *ethos* was determined by a combination of Enlightenment rationalism of the type of Jefferson with free church conviction. Both espoused the separation of church and state. Revolution was not made simply for a utopian idea but practically for the natural rights of man. At the same time, the sense of human wickedness present in the New England Calvinist background led to the distrust of any single ruler. The divine right of kings was unthinkable. Accepted instead was the insight of the Hebrew prophets that beyond men and nations is a higher judgment and righteousness. At the same time, it was recognized that faith in God cannot be imposed from without.

Bellah points out that the supporters of slavery before the Civil War came to reject the *ethos* of the Declaration of Independence. Some of the more consistent ones attacked not only Jeffersonian democracy but Reformation religion, dreaming of medieval chivalry and the divine right of monarchy. The legacy of Jefferson and Lincoln does not make for intolerance. Today, the religious consensus it expresses remains important as the United States has taken on a larger role in international relations in the era of the two world wars.

Bellah believes that every president since Franklin Roosevelt has been groping toward a new pattern of action in the world while still seeking to preserve, to use a phrase of Kennedy, "the revolutionary beliefs for which our forebearers fought."[22] Without an awareness that the nation stands under a higher judgment, American national policy becomes dangerous. The biblical archetypes, The Exodus, chosen people, Promised Land, New Jerusalem, sacrificial death and rebirth, are deeply ingrained in the nation's history and consciousness. The nation itself has not been worshiped. Instead, there has been a common concern that America be a society as perfectly in accord with the will of God as men can make it, a light to all nations.

Some presidents more than others have attempted to understand the American experience in the light of ultimate and universal reality. Some more than others, Lincoln for example, have shown themselves capable of growth. The presence of religious loyalty did not remove moral ambiguity or make decisions for them. However, it has given them depth as well as abiding relevance.

During the 1976 election campaign, the question of religious beliefs was raised by audiences, not just by candidates. Hearers would not allow it to be shunted aside with a *pro forma* answer. Why was this the case?

Malachi B. Martin finds: "There is a deep persuasion among the people that the moral conscience bred by religious faith is as much a fundamental part of the American heritage as the laws and the Constitution."[23]

Washington in his Farewell Address cited such a common sense:

> Of all the dispositions and habits which leads to political prosperity, Religion and Morality are indispensable supports. . . . Whatever may be conceded to the influence of refined education on minds of peculiar structure, reason and experience both forbid us to expect that National morality can prevail in exclusion of religious principle.[24]

THEOLOGICAL GROUNDS

The religious traditions of the presidency become clearer by contrast with those of monarchy. The role of the Christian king was a determining one throughout a millenium and a half of European history, ever since Constantine's conversion to Christianity. Caesaro-papism, Caesar ruling in the Church, began its long history with this monarch. Partly in reaction against it, there was a long struggle between church and state in the Middle Ages. The religious and political were conceived as separate and conflicting realms. Pope was pitted against emperor in the struggle between two sovereigns.

The religion of the presidency began a new tradition—not an exclusively secular one. Liberty of worship was regarded as a right of conscience; no ruler can dictate personal belief about God and human destiny. The intent of the Founding Fathers was freedom for rather than freedom from religion. The tradition of the presidency can be summed up by saying that both church and state are responsible to God directly. Although both religious and political communities exist side by side in the same population, they are not identical. Nor is their relation hierarchical; the state need not proceed through the church to deity. Political life should conform to God's commands, but these are not mediated for the state by any religious institution or church authority.

At times, more secularist views have been honored. These have interpreted democracy as an end in itself, without responsibility to God. In times of crisis, especially, and with the concerns and burdens of the presidency, they have not been predominant. Finally, the issues of history, good and evil, life and death, cannot be ignored. Political power is not just its own end but must serve higher purposes of human welfare. The duty to uphold liberty, equality, and justice, which falls on the president, roots finally in ultimate values. Persons are worthy of dignity and respect because of the rights given to them by their Creator. The humanitarian concerns of the presidency, its idealism and commitment to serve the people have a religious basis. In affirming it, President Carter is not an outsider to the traditions of his office.

4. The Shadow of Watergate

WATERGATE AND THE CAMPAIGN

Jimmy Carter's candidacy and election would have taken a very different form without the Watergate incident. Formally announcing his candidacy on December 12, 1974, Carter said:

> Recently we have discovered that our trust has been betrayed. The veils of secrecy have seemed to thicken around Washington. The purposes and goals of our country are uncertain and sometimes even suspect. Our people are understandably concerned with this lack of competence and integrity. . . . With the shame of Watergate still with us and our 200th birthday just ahead, it is time for us to reaffirm and to strengthen our ethical and spiritual and political beliefs.[1]

Watergate was not just a personal tragedy for Richard Nixon, the first president of the United States to resign in personal disgrace. It was a moral and religious crisis of the first order. Nixon was not a tyrant who had come to power by force or revolution. Twice he had been elected vice president and twice president in open democratic elections. His first ascent to the White House had been by a very slim popular majority. The second victory was with a wide margin. Already during the campaign, while giving external signs of piety and righteousness, the incumbent president had used the machinery of government to conceal evidence about the Watergate break-in. The revelation of the facts, together with his real-life attitudes, came about because a very modern technological device had been installed in his office. Television has changed national politics; so, too, have tape recorders. The June 23rd conversations were the conclusive proof that Nixon had lied.

Nixon's name remained unmentioned at the 1976 Republican Convention. His successor, Gerald Ford, claimed to have brought a new spirit to the White House. Ford's pardon of the former president, like Watergate, was in the background of the campaign even when not explicitly debated. Nixon resigned without repentance. At that time, a Senate resolution recommending that he be exempted from legal action against him was withdrawn after he refused any acknowledgement of guilt. He had deceived others. He had deceived himself. Nixon's enemies had long charged that he was a dishonest and conniving person. "Tricky Dicky," they had dubbed him. But does not a candidate who endures the fury of political controversy on the way to the presidency reflect the selfish concerns as well as the idealism of the country? Was this not the case, even as Watergate was taking place?

NIXON'S USE OF POWER

The outcome of the 1972 campaign against the Democratic candidate, George McGovern, need never have been in doubt. The Republican victory was an easy one. Yet the president and his advisors misjudged matters badly. The Watergate scandal made clear for all to see, his glaring inability to gather together really competent advisors who were men of integrity and sound judgment. Nixon may not have been informed in advance of the Watergate break-in, but he had countenanced strategies such as were employed by the Plumbers group. His ruthlessness was well known to his associates. White House complicity in the break-in was covered up during the campaign. Nixon had claimed good intentions; he had not refused the plaudits of piety. His national stature was enhanced by his association with religious leaders such as Billy Graham. The result was that many persons concluded a president who prays must be honest. Still, religion is not a blank check for truthfulness but needs to be viewed critically. There is hardly any evil that has not at one time or another been sanctified by piety: slavery, the Crusades, the divine right of kings. One need not be religious to tell the truth; that is just common decency. Separation of church and state is designed to prevent religious sanction for political abuse, but it does not absolve a president claiming to believe in God from responsibility to Him and to His laws.

Special Prosecutor Leon Jaworski, in his book, *The Right and the Power,* concludes: ''The teachings of right and wrong were forgotten in the White House.''[2] Little evils grew into great ones; small sins escalated into big ones. Jaworski listened to hours and hours of tapes, but never once heard a reference to the glory of God or spiritual guidance through prayer. ''Our Lord was mentioned, yes, but on each pitiable occasion His name was taken in vain.'' If only he could have heard an occasional prayer for help, an occasional show of compassion, he exclaims, or just the simple statement, '' 'may we hold our honor sacred.' . . . . How different might have been the course of government if there had been an acknowledgement of God as the source of right instead of denial of Him in a seemingly unending series of ruthless actions.''

Power in itself is not wrong or inevitably corrupting. The basic moral issue is how it is used. For Nixon, it had become an end in itself. What one hears in listening to the tapes is really Machiavellian. The end justifies the means. Power alone remains to be reckoned with and is used cynically and ruthlessly. In such circumstances, the issue of character cannot be avoided.

Publicly, Nixon was moralistic and pious. Privately the tapes show him to be vain, profane, and cynical. There was a fatal flaw in the man's person which opened him to his enemies and cost him his high office. Theodore H. White, in *Breach of Faith,* commented: "The true crime of Richard Nixon was simple: he destroyed the myth that binds America together, and for this he was driven from power."[3] That myth, White believes, is that somewhere in American life there is at least one man who stands for law—the president.

PRAYER AND PIETY

Only a few new episodes were added to the record of Watergate by Bob Woodward and Carl Bernstein's book, *The Final Days.*[4] One of them is the prayer scene: Woodard and Bernstein report that Nixon asked Henry Kissinger to pray with him. He was not sure that he had the strength to be the first president of the United States to resign. "Will history treat me more kindly than my contemporaries?" Nixon asked, as tears flooded his eyes. What had he done to the country or its people? How could it be so torn apart by a simple burglary, a breaking and entering? Nixon is supposed to have said, "Henry, you are not a very orthodox Jew and I am not an orthodox Quaker, but we need to pray." When the president kneeled down, the Secretary of

State did so as well. Nixon prayed out loud, asking God for help, rest, peace, and love. Then, sobbing, he leaned over and struck his fist on the carpet and cried out, "What have I done? What has happened?" Woodard and Bernstein report that Kissinger touched the president, trying to console him, "to bring rest and peace to the man who was curled on the carpet like a child." In his own thoughts, the Secretary of State was certain the president would never escape the verdict of Watergate.

Nixon had sanctioned the wide use of prayer from the outset of his term as president. A religious observance committee worked for months in advance to set a spiritual tone for his first inaugural.[5] Before the ceremony, it requested all churches and synagogues to unite in prayer for the new president, for the government, and for the country. On the day itself, a collection of prayers, Bible readings, and famous quotations was distributed. Ten thousand specially printed cards depicted a pair of hands in an attitude of prayer with the words, "Thanksgiving, Blessing, Dedication, Guidance." Billy Graham opened the inaugural with a prayer. Nixon's address itself was replete with references to God and the Bible. "Spiritual heritage" was Nixon's key word, but there was nothing Christian in his usage.[6] It is not too much to say that he was easily drawn to the simplistic, mythical imagination.

The tragedy was that Nixon simply did not understand what the Bible teaches about God's judgment on men and nations. Accordingly, he linked America's strength to its power and delimited the American dream simply as including the benefits of religion.

Garry Wills believes that when Nixon preached "faith in America," he tested his faith in the final analysis on the affirmation that there is no limit to what man can achieve. He only must use his intelligence, his technocracy, and his ideals. Nixon not only overlooked the tragedy of the human condition, but had no sense of grace or justification by faith.

Henderson concludes in criticism:

Nixon systematically appropriates the vocabulary of the church—faith, trust, hope, belief, spirit—and applies these words not to a transcendent God but to his own nation.[7]

He appealed to his personal vision of what it should be. Refusing to recognize any corrupting self-interest, he claimed a free hand, ranging around the world. Lacking a transcendent God, Nixon made patriotism his religion, the American dream his deity. He did not return to "spiritual sources" that made the nation great as he claimed. Instead, he accomplished "a macabre reversal of those traditions, selling the mirror image as the original."

NIXON'S CHARACTER

The search for the real Richard Nixon began long before Watergate. Even as he was ruthless in political in-fighting, Nixon saw himself as virtuous. Newsmen disliked his unctuous style. He tended to see crucial events as personal crises and tests of his will and strength. The evidence is clear that he engendered a ruthless atmosphere of partisanship in his immediate circle. Watergate was a revelation of this style of leadership. Increasingly, in the midst of Watergate, he isolated himself with a barrier of protective aids and would shrink from face-to-face encounter. At the same time, he was badly served by men who had no higher loyalty than himself. Everyone in leading positions in government and society who did not wear his brand was regarded as suspect.

Mazlish in his 1972 book, *In Search of Nixon,* attempted an analysis of the President's character.[8] He emphasized three outstanding personality traits: Nixon had a unique absorption of self in his role. Although he did not always recognize it, to "Be Himself" is always to be the particular role in which he finds himself. "Nixon is his role." Mazlish identifies Nixon's second outstanding trait as ambivalence. The trait is present in all men in some measure. But Mazlish claims never to have dealt with a public figure as ambivalent as Richard Nixon. A third trait, clearly related to this ambivalence, is denial. "Nixon uses mammoth denial as a defense against unacceptable impulses and feelings." He simply refused to recognize his own aggressive intent. He constantly said things like, "I don't say this bitterly," when it was transparently clear that he is bitter. Mazlish believes that there is nothing wrong with being bitter sometimes! Inability to recognize one's own baser impulses and to seek forgiveness or release, only perpetuates them. In theological terms, sin feeds on the desire to "play God," rather than acknowledge one's mistakes.

A president's character significantly determines the attitudes of his associates; Nixon was not only aloof and secretive, but obsessed with concern about how he would meet crises. It is clear that the White House was seriously out of touch with reality. Even though Nixon occupied the seat of national power, he felt weak and defensive. Watergate followed!

Mazlish judged that what observers often took for a lack of conviction was in fact an obsession with contradictory roles of the moment. Nixon, he believes, looked for security in the roles he played. It is too simple to say that he was without idealism. Nixon wanted to make a place for himself in history like Wilson, DeGaulle, or Churchill. His drive was not just for power but for respect and fame.

The chief executive is both arbiter and interpreter of

destiny, a role that is not achieved without power or the struggle for it. A basic moral and even religious question is how the chief executive regards power. Some presidents have recognized and welcomed its presence. Others have been reluctant to accept it. Biographers report that both of the Roosevelts, Theodore and Franklin, enjoyed the struggle of political life, finding it productive of personal fulfillment. General Eisenhower is reported to have sought high office, but to have attempted to stand above conflict after he had achieved power.

One political scientist, Erwin C. Hargrove, believes Nixon yearned for regularity and order in government. He feels that Nixon had a strong personal desire to be a passive president who would reign over a happy people in a tension-free time. In such a setting, he might receive all the adulation and deference that he conceived to be his due. "Such a dream, if realized, would finally free Richard Nixon from the phantoms that drive him."[9]

But this does not come to pass in the real world. Nixon oscillated between a kind of quietism and appeal to good will and unity and an activist testing of opposition. There is evidence in the tapes to support the claim that Nixon was haunted by an adversary situation, real and imagined. His self-image was that of a man beleaguered by his enemies. This was part of his character and is not unrelated to his ultimate life values. What were his real convictions?

The office of the presidency is heavy with symbolism and influence. Increasingly it lives more under the shadow of Hamilton than of Jefferson. Today, strong and active leadership is required. Presidents have to make decisions and take strong actions when others cannot or will not. More and more problems have come to be thrust upon the office—during the depression, the Second World War, and the cold war.

The president of the United States has been described as

the most powerful person in the world. On his personal command, the atomic and hydrogen bomb destruction of a large part of civilization could take place in only a few moments. A president ought to be of sound jugment as well as impeccable character. Watergate was more than a single lie. It was a revelation of cynicism and bad faith. The lesson is moralistically simple, that when public officials lie, one deception leads to another. There is no substitute for integrity in government. We cannot expect to know fully in advance what a political leader will do in every circumstance. But we can expect honesty.

ANALYZING PRESIDENTIAL CHARACTER

Carter has described James David Barber's study, *Presidential Character,* as the best book on the office that he has ever read. Barber observes: ''Political power is like nuclear energy: available to create deserts or make them bloom.''[10] He uses four classifications to describe past chief executives: Positive/Active, Positive/Passive, Negative/Active, and Negative/Passive. He classifies Richard Nixon as an Active/Negative type. Barber suggests four tests for a prospective president to be: a healthy confidence in self, ability to communicate with the public, capacity to negotiate close up with other politicians, and finally, a mastery of details and general policy. In Barber's judgment, Carter has a good chance of turning out to be an Active/Positive president.

The first section of the book tells three tragic tales of earlier Active/Negative presidents: Woodrow Wilson, failing in his goal to involve the United States in the League of Nations, Herbert Hoover, who lost office because of the depression, and Lyndon Johnson, rendered powerless and renouncing public office amid the war in Vietnam. All three were overcome by situations they helped to create. The office had "gotten to them," wearing them down so that they acted out of compulsion. Finally, however, according to Barber, they failed because of flaws in their character. Barber lists as Passive/Negative presidents, Calvin Coolidge and Dwight Eisenhower, and as Passive/Positive ones, Theodore Roosevelt and William Howard Taft. Not as energetic as others, they were yet affirmative. Barber's study is detailed. A summary of his classification cannot do full justice to the many faceted richness of his description.

Barber's most laudatory category is Active/Positive. He is careful not to assign a common mold to all presidents he designates in this way. Characteristically, however, he emphasizes that they did rise to the circumstances of the time: Franklin Roosevelt to the crises of the depression and the Second World War, Harry Truman to the problems of post-war Europe, and John F. Kennedy to the urgency of racial integration. Responding positively personally, they gave meaningful and effective leadership in time of need. Working hard, they found the holding of power conducive to personal fulfillment.

PREDICTING PRESIDENTIAL CHARACTER

Can presidential character be predicted? Writing in 1972, Barber did an amazing analysis of the problems of Richard Nixon's personal life, soon to be revealed by the Watergate tapes.

Barber boldly states: "The presidency exists solely in the minds of men."[11] The institution is "nothing more than images, habits, and intentions shared by the humans who make it up and by those who react to them." The American people fear two dangers, he points out: pride and perfidy. Pride appears as a danger when a president seems to be pushing too hard and too fast, without proper consultation.

Perfidy is a kind of characterological betrayal: a president breaks trust in the image of his office as dignified, episcopal, plain and clean in character.

Some of Barber's remarks assuredly have influenced Carter, and they seem to be prophetic of the president's own statements. For example, Barber has written: "Beside a candid confession of failure, presidential leadership today must remind citizens that their past was not without achievement and that their future is not yet spoiled." He ends his book on a populist more than an academic theme: leadership should reawaken convictions momentarily buried in fear and mistrust. It need not just conjure up sentiments. "A presidential character who can see beyond tomorrow—and smile—might yet lead us out of the wilderness."[12]

5. Black and White Together

CARTER CAMPAIGNING

Carter had a long and tiring day of campaigning. It began at the U.S. Steel Homestead works in the Pittsburgh area, just after 6:00 A.M. Then he made a trip down into a coal mine at Finleyville, appeared before students at Duquesne University and responded on a call-in radio talk show. Nonetheless, he arrived punctually and even a bit ahead of schedule for a speech to a group of black voters in a politically neglected corner of Pittsburgh. Motivated by his belief that he has special empathy with blacks, Carter included more meetings with them than any other major candidate during the primaries. He was introduced by two politicians and a football player, J. T. Thomas, the defensive back for the Pittsburgh Steelers. Carter's speech at the Carnegie Branch Library can be fairly described as spellbinding. Speaking with his shirt sleeves rolled up, he described the passage of the Civil Rights Acts as ''the best thing that ever happened to the South. . . . . They liberated whites as well as blacks.''[1] Then he recounted how a portrait of Martin Luther King, Jr. was placed in the Georgia state capitol building during his term as governor.

Apologizing for his "ethnic purity" line, Carter emphasized his belief that "not only do blacks have a right to equality, but blacks are equal." He explained that now his eight-year-old daughter, Amy, attends the public school at Plains, Georgia and has no idea how many children in her class are whites or blacks. Carter ended with rhetorical hyperbole, "I would rather die than disappoint Andrew Young or Martin Luther King, Sr. or Coleman Young." Congressman Andrew Young had been one of the black politicians who had introduced him.

Carter's childhood life in the cotton fields was recounted many times during the campaign.[2] He has said that when he was young, almost all of his playmates were black. They worked together, hunted, fished, and swam together. "But when it was time for church or for school, we went our separate ways, without really understanding why." Unspoken, unwritten, but powerful rules, were almost never challenged. Jimmy's father, Mr. Earl, provided food, clothing, and money for his dependent blacks. But he kept them separate from the whites except when they were working together in the cotton fields.

As a candidate, Carter went after the black vote in face-to-face encounter in state after state, appearing at schools and churches, on street corners, and in community halls. Representative Yvonne Burke, Chairperson of the Black Congressional Caucus, explains, "He goes into black communities and he involves black people."[3] Carter's ability to understand and to relate to their view of the world is very evident. He asked that his black audience join his "family" and his "crusade" for the presidency.

After his address in Pittsburgh, he answered a few questions and prepared to leave. However, before he could depart, a heavy-set middle aged man at the front of the room started shouting about tokenism and barred the way. "The people out here aren't given a chance," he cried, referring to the black neighborhoods. Others affirmed his claim, shouting, ''Amen.'' Tension increased as a woman in the rear of the room strutted back and forth waving her scarf and yelling, ''Now let's talk about the real issues. . . . . Let's make him answer the questions.'' Although the chairman could not control the crowd, Carter listened patiently. Then he remarked, ''I'm not in favor of tokenism either.'' Immediately, it became clear that the man in front was on Carter's side after all as he thanked ''the only candidate to show his face in this neighborhood.'' Carter leaped off the stage smiling and bounded his way through the crowd. He shook hands and hugged persons along the way as he left.

CARTER'S CAREER

The fact that Carter's mother did not conform fully to the segregationist mores of the rural South has received attention. She told her children to address their black elders as Uncle and Aunt and barred the use of the word ''nigger.'' When she welcomed a black bishop's yankee-educated son to coffee in her living room, her husband left discreetly. Carter describes her as working twelve hours a day or even twenty, as a registered nurse, and then coming home to care for her family.[4] She served people, black and white alike. Carter writes that she knew no color line. ''Her black friends were just as welcome in our home as her white friends, a fact that shocked some people, sometimes even my father, who was very conventional then in his views on race.'' Still, the Baptist Church and the stumpy three-car Butt Head, the train on which the family travelled to Archery and Americus was segregated. Blacks and whites did not ride together.

When A. D. Davis was hired to baby-sit for Jimmy's younger brother, Billy, he was more or less incorporated into the family. He even sat with him downstairs at the movies until feeling ill at ease, he would sneak away to the black balcony of the Rylander Theater. When Carter was asked what was his biggest mistake, he replied, "Oh, back in the late forties I was reluctant to yield to black people their equality of opportunities. I got over that." Carter claims to know black people so well because he has lived with them, played with them, fished with them, and worked with them. He rowed the same boats, hunted birds behind the same dogs, and when civil rights legislation was passed, he didn't have to walk across the street and say "Hi, I'm Jimmy Carter. I've been your neighbor for the last forty-one years." He affirms: "I have known black people and they know me."

During his career as a naval officer, Carter and a black submarine shipmate were nearly asphyxiated together as they tried to fix a short-circuited battery amid a billow of toxic fumes. Returning to Plains after his discharge, he did not join the White Citizens' Council or acquiesce in the continued segregation of the Plains Baptist Church. Carter did vote for a segregationist amendment to the Georgia constitution while in the state senate, but opposed the notorious thirty questions. The latter was a virtually impossible literacy test designed to keep blacks from voting. Carter encouraged Wallace and Maddox support for himself in his race for the governorship against Carl Sanders. He had promised black civil rights leaders in Atlanta to be a color blind governor, but had added, "You won't like my campaign." Inaugurated as governor, his position was clear. He said in his inaugural speech:

> I believe I know our people as well as anyone. Based on this knowledge of Georgians, north and south, rural and urban, liberal and conservative, I say to you quite frankly that the time for racial discrimination is over. Our people have already made

this major and difficult decision, but we cannot underestimate the challenge of hundreds of minor decisions.

. . . No poor, rural, weak, or black person should ever have to bear the additional burden of being deprived of the opportunity of an education, a job or simple justice. . . . As governor, I will never shirk this responsibility.[5]

Subsequently, the Ku Klux Klan paraded outside while Martin Luther King, Jr.'s portrait together with that of two other black Georgians was hung in the Statehouse.

Wesley Pippert, who covered Carter for United Press International during the presidential campaign, urged that it is important to research his relations with blacks.[6] Why is he unique, so unlike his neighbors? More than a decade ago, he urged the integration of the Plains Baptist Church when most other ''born again'' people feared it. The processes by which Carter integrated his personal trust in God with his political tactics are not fully transparent. He comes from the black belt country, a hotbed of resistance to the civil rights movement. It is too easily forgotten that the cities nearest to Plains, Albany and Americus, jailed Martin Luther King, Jr. Why did Carter become politically active toward the poor, blacks, and other racial minorities who are distinguished by speaking a foreign language?

THE BLACK REVOLUTION

Consideration of the religious bases and implications of Carter's present stand must begin with an appraisal of the situation of the blacks as well as the relation of the Christian ideal of equality to it. Daniel Thompson in his study, *The Negro Leadership Class,* develops a threefold typology: (1) Uncle Tom, (2) the racial diplomat, and (3) the race man. Color caste was enforced by slavery in the plantation era.[7] It continued after the Civil War in the Uncle Tom pattern. Blacks were forced to accept this status in the segregation pattern of the post-slavery South. The dominant symbol was Booker T. Washington. Then, about the turn of the century, this approach was replaced by that of the racial diplomat-type which remained dominant until after the Second World War.

Today, caste discrimination has been attacked by black leaders, often motivated by a heightened sense of ethnocentrism. In fact, a revolution has taken place in the black self-image. All sense of shame for color or race is rightly refused. During the Second World War, more than a million blacks from both North and South served in the armed forces. The conviction that they were fighting for democracy made any racial discrimination intolerable. Of crucial importance was the 1954 Supreme Court decision in the case of *Brown vs. Board of Education*. The Justices stated: "We conclude that in the field of public education the doctrine of 'separate but equal' has no place. *Separate educational facilities are inherently unequal.*"

Unfortunately, the full benefits of integration have often been limited to a relatively narrow and select group of blacks in the talented middle class. Economic and social problems continue, too often with a sense of apathy, in the urban ghettos.

Black leaders have an uncompromising determination that the members of their community will decide who they are and what they will do. Ethnocentric solidarity means that blacks do not want to be assimilated benevolently into white communities. Instead, they seek their own rights and political power. Personal goodness is not enough. Charity will not do. The dynamic of change which led to such convictions was effective in the North and West before the South. Legal segregation did not exist in these regions. The so-called Great Migration out of the South had begun even by the First World War. By 1960, seventy-two percent of the non-whites were living in urban areas. The dynamic of change has finally reached to Plains, Georgia.

MARTIN LUTHER KING, JR.

Carter continues to speak in eulogy of Martin Luther King, Jr. Courageously attacking ideologies of both black and white supremacy, King was outspokenly Christian and opposed violence. "I think you can be militantly non-violent," he said.[8] King's strategy, in his non-violent fight for civil rights, was one of direct action to mobilize the black masses on specific issues. At the same time, he appealed to the conscience of liberal whites. He looked to the moral power of an aroused white America to support change. Focusing on the concrete social problem of de-segregation, he achieved success. Although King opposed violence, he nonetheless believed that dignity could come to blacks only as they have enough power to demand reform for themselves. While he was concerned that blacks move ahead on their own, his outlook was not secessionist but assimilationist. Basically, he wished them to be a part of American society, but with political equality and equality of opportunity. The sense of inferiority and futility among blacks must be overcome.

Martin Luther King, Sr. has said of Carter, "I know what he is and what he stands for. . . . I'm with him all the way."[9] King not only has refuted charges that Carter is a racist and liar, but he described the presidential candidate as one of his closest friends and one of the finest governors Georgia ever had. Full page advertisements of King's endorsement were run in black community newspapers and sixty second radio spots purchased on black stations across the country. The endorsement of Congressman Andrew

Young was also very important strategically. Bode notes pointedly: "George Wallace is the main reason Jimmy Carter has drawn so strongly among blacks."[10]

It has been said that the only person to whom Carter owes a political debt is Congressman Andrew Young. Whatever the truth of the claim, there could hardly be a more decent politician for such an obligation. Young has consistently urged that politics must not be determined from black special interest or power, but must reflect national goals and welfare. Carter's election would have been impossible without his own linking of blacks and rednecks in what Orde Coombs has called "the grand coalition of '76." Young did not back Carter in either of his gubernatorial races. He explains his position, "Wallace pulled the whole Democratic party to the right. To get the country moving again, Wallacism had to be stopped in the South, where it started. The defeat of George Wallace may end up being the defeat of overt political racism in America."[11]

Julian Bond, a black Democratic member of the Georgia Senate, refused to support Carter; he disagrees with Young. He stated: "Carter is getting the black vote by default, and it is wholly undeserved."[12] Bond argued that there is no ideological reason to justify such support. He concluded that voters have evidently stopped making decisions in terms of racial self-interest, welfare, unemployment, housing, and crime in the streets. "Carter is not being judged in political terms or in civil rights terms. He's simply being perceived as a good person and a Christian."

Coles points out, in rebuttal, that Carter has earned the trust and confidence not only of Andrew Young and Martin Luther King, Sr., but on the white side such men as Charles Morgan who for years has been an American Civil Liberties attorney in the Southeast.[13] These are the most honorable and fearless people of the region, not fools, nor are they taken in by rhetorical flourishes or pietistic drivel. Coles contends:

> Their support for Jimmy Carter is essentially pragmatic, unsentimental, and in the non-pejorative sense of the word calculating. . . . As for the blacks, they knew that upon his election as governor of Georgia Jimmy Carter began to deliver the goods quickly and persistently, against substantial odds.

THE CHRISTIAN ETHIC

It is important to look at the religious issue very carefully. Ernst Troeltsch in his classic, *The Social Teachings of the Christian Churches,* argues that Christianity does not yield a social ethic as such.[14] However, when it calls on individuals to manifest love toward each other, ''all earthly distinctions are swallowed up in the Divine power and love which reduce all other distinctions to nothing.'' The Christian Gospel teaches that each man is related to God through divine grace. The state of being in Christ is one of brotherhood. Grace creates a community of men equal in their freedom. Equality is before God, not merely man. Troeltsch argues that the idea of equality is intrinsic to Christianity as a system of absolute value which is both universalistic and individualistic. The social ideals of universalism, individualism, equality, and freedom are all implicit as well as interrelated in its Gospel. They require each other. God's activity is that of creative love; freedom is one of its socio-political characteristics. Christian individualism is a radical individualism; it affirms that those who are related to God are related equally to Him. Christianity is concerned for both order and justice. Currently, the phenomenon of racial discrimination cannot be appraised apart from the Christian doctrine of sin. Sin as pride leads men to refuse to admit their finiteness in the pretensions of racial idolatry.

At the beginning of the fourth quarter of the last century, Rutherford B. Hayes betrayed the rights of the newly freed slaves in order to win an election. They were left to the terror of the Ku Klux Klan. A hundred years later, Carter has reversed the pattern in an alliance of born-again whites and Bible-quoting blacks—the so-called holy alliance of '76. Events might have been foreseen from what the novelist, William Faulkner, wrote in 1949. He had one of his white protagonists say of black people: ''We—he and us—should confederate: swap him the rest of the economic and cultural privileges which are his right.''[15] No longer expected just to wait and endure and survive, blacks with whites would prevail, ''together we would dominate the United States.'' Faulkner's protagonist explains that together they would be impregnable, unthreatened ''by a mass of people who no longer have anything in common save a frantic greed for money and a basic fear of a failure of national character.''

PLAINS, GEORGIA

Halloween, Sunday, October 31, 1976, two days before the presidential election, the service in the Plains Baptist Church was cancelled. There would be no public worship that week. The minister, the Reverend Bruce Edwards, stood before its locked doors. He explained that he had urged the deacons to open the doors and to allow the Rev. Clennon King of Albany, Georgia, and three other blacks to attend. The Sunday earlier, he had endorsed the integration of the church on Christian principles. Clennon King, no relation to the Martin Luther King, had run for president in

1960, on the Afro-American ticket and again in 1972, as an Independent. Miss Lillian said that she would not remain in the church if membership were denied solely because of race. King does not live in Plains.

Miss Lillian gave the congregation and the deacons the benefit of the doubt by saying: ''I know that if any other black who was decent wanted to come into the church they would welcome him.'' Sunday, November 14, 1976, in a secret ballot, the congregation voted to integrate. It may only have been the beginning of new problems; the decision was not won without division. But a significant victory had been achieved. No doubt, the president-elect had used his influence, for the benefit of the Plains church and the country!

The unhappy fact is that Amy Carter meets her black playmates not at the Baptist Church but at school. Churches with congregational government are much more difficult to integrate than public schools, as Carter learned to his pain. But racial discrimination is a moral and religious issue, a clear violation of the Christian commandment to love. Christian faith in an all-loving God provides the basis for a higher universal loyalty. Carter understands it is necessary to go beyond restraining man's sin to claim a more fully human life. What is God doing in the world? The Christian answer is that he is creating a new humanity—in the Christian Church. Christianity is not just otherworldly. It brings new fellowship in an I-Thou relation. Certain minimum rights can be established by law, but the brotherhood for which Carter appeals is more difficult. Carter comments of blacks:

> They care for me and I care for them. We have a lot in common, a belief in one another. We share a common faith in Christ. We speak the same language. We sing the same hymns. We've

seen the same poverty and the same disease. We've seen the same struggles in the South and the same growth. We've overcome the same obstacles. It has bound us together in the spirit of brotherhood and love.[16]

The state by judicial and police power has been able to affect what the churches have too often failed to do in their own ranks. Racism is sin. Yet reform has had religious inspiration from a host of courageous leaders, black and white, symbolized by Martin Luther King, Jr. Racial prejudice and hatred cannot be destroyed by political sanction alone. Carter has not avoided the ethical issue, yet at the same time has recognized that change must have a basis in political power. To fault him simply because he is not unqualifiedly a liberal is too simple. Coles points out that ''Carter keeps reminding his audience in a courteous, soft, unassuming accent, the South's black and white people know one another well.''[17] Today they often send their children to the same schools. They appear to be less angry or nasty with each other than people in Boston, Massachusetts, for example. Coles concludes: ''The Georgian comes across to many as proud of his country as well as critical of it. . . .''

6. Honesty and Power in Foreign Policy

OPENNESS

Carter's foreign policy statements have reflected his ethical and religious concerns. Clearly, he gives priority to openness and respect for human rights. Carter was asked about past practices and policy. How did he explain all those deceptions and secret maneuverings during the years? Why were they allowed to happen? Carter replied that it was a matter of people's just saying, "Well, that's politics."[1] They did not insist on the right to know what the government was doing. Secrecy is O.K., accepting gifts O.K., excluding the American people O.K.

Carter has not used cold war jargon in speaking of international relations. At the same time he has refused communism, he has criticized the Nixon ideology. For example, he singled out the pretext of national security as it was used to conceal information from the American public. Such devices make doubly evident why no man should be allowed to become all powerful. Carter stated:

> Kissinger has been in the position of being almost uniquely a spokesman for our nation. I think that it is a legitimate role and

a proper responsibility of the President himself. Kissinger has had a kind of Lone Ranger, secret foreign-policy attitude, which almost ensures that there cannot be adequate consultation with our allies; there cannot be a long-range commitment to unchanging principles; there cannot be a coherent evolution on foreign policy; there cannot be a bipartisan approach with support and advice from Congress. This is what I would avoid as President and is one of the major defects in the Nixon-Ford foreign policy as expressed by Kissinger.[2]

Fearing a lack of support among the State Department staff, Nixon and his Secretary of State concentrated all power among themselves at the top. Even when Kissinger worked eighteen hours a day, he could not deal with all problems adequately. The normal working of the State Department was reduced to impotence, awaiting higher directives from him. Day to day diplomacy was often displaced by crisis, vest pocket negotiations. Carter has not argued that a negotiator must show all of his cards openly in advance, leaving himself no options. Yet he knows a constitutional democracy does require openness of policy. Without public confidence in the good faith of its government, diplomacy collapses. Kissinger was strikingly successful in the opening to China. His statecraft was a failure in Vietnam. A sense of deception and mistrust on the part of Congress and the public led them to refuse support for his policy in Angola. When he could not deliver what he had threatened and promised there, foreign ambassadors asked whether American leadership could be trusted at all.

PRESIDENTIAL LEADERSHIP

A number of considerations support Carter's view that the president himself must be in charge of foreign policy. International and domestic pressures overlap. Foreign relations can no longer be isolated from domestic issues as much as in the nineteenth century. Whatever happens on one continent affects others, often almost immediately, whether it be in science, economics, police control of terrorism, or ideology. No single department of government, state, defense, commerce, or agriculture can correlate all factors. None is fully free of self-interest. Even the State Department reflects its own particular concerns and prejudices. Responsibility to make and to coordinate foreign policy falls on the president.

Carter believes that a diplomacy which compromises right and wrong is self-defeating. He has said that as president he would never intervene in order to overthrow a government. He would use prestige, legitimate diplomatic leverage, and trade mechanisms, if enough were at stake for American national interest. But he would not undertake efforts that would be embarrassing to the United States if they were revealed completely. Carter noted that in a speech Kissinger said Brazil is the sort of government that is most compatible with that of the United States. Carter reacted: "Well, that's the kind of thing we want to change."[3] Carter recognizes that Brazil is a military dictatorship. In many instances, it is highly repressive to political prisoners. Earlier foreign policy has sometimes short-circuited moral principles for temporary advantage. Carter finds that in every instance it has been counter productive. When the CIA undertakes covert activities that might be justified if they were peaceful, the nation always suffers in influence and prestige.

Carter affirms that the United States must seek justice in a sinful world more aggressively out of concern for other people's freedom and welfare. Of course, the fact that great powers struggle together in defense of their own self-interest cannot be changed simply by idealism. Yet a cynical version of self-interest, explicit or implicit, is all too easily recognized for what it is. Secrecy and violence are self-defeating. Kissinger's secret shuttle diplomacy has been dramatic, giving priority to quick results. Its demand for immediate success can play into the hands of the other side when an opponent can wait out events as in Vietnam. Reform like respect for human rights has often come too late under Kissinger. A lack of responsiveness to human need has hurt the United States.

Carter understands that it is naive to suppose that communism is the only enemy. He accepts a limited policy of détente but remarks: "As I've said in my speeches, I feel that a policy of *détente has given up too much to the Russians and gotten too little in return."* 4 Carter believes that Kissinger has too often equated his own popularity with the so-called advantages of détente. *World leaders feel the United States has abandoned a long-standing principle of mutual consultation and sharing of responsibility for problems. Carter also wishes to have stronger bilateral relations with the developing nations.*

NIXON'S COLD WAR POLICY

Carter is sure that the best answer to communism is the establishment of justice, freedom, and democracy. This did not come about in Vietnam. Military strategies do not necessarily promote political solutions.

Charles Henderson, in *The Nixon Theology,* finds a tragic paradox at the heart of Nixon's policy, promoting himself as at once a pacifist and a cold warrior. He believes there was no chance for a just peace in Vietnam after so many years of the most terrible crimes—both the continuing mass violence of American bombings and the selective terror of the Vietcong. Peace alone would be a gift of grace, the least of evils; continuation of the war was the greatest evil. "That Nixon can achieve justice in Vietnam is a suggestion perverse in its impossibility."[5] Bribery and murder had become routine in the land.

Carter has said of Vietnam:

> The American people were tremendously misled about the immediate prospects for victory, about the level of our involvement, about the relative cost in American lives. If I had known in the Sixties what I knew in the early Seventies, I think I would have spoken out more strongly.[6]

Nixon came to power in the era of the cold war, espousing a radical dualism, light and dark, good and evil. This outlook was, to say the least, simplistic. Carter does not share it. Nixon's early approach to the Russians was expressed in his now famous Kitchen Debate with Premier Khrushchev. He had already taken on the Premier aggressively even before their public confrontation at Sokolnika Park. While a dinner guest, he protested about anti-American propaganda in Russia. The vice president even involved the wives in the argument. Throughout his tour in the Soviet Union, he found the Communists to be miniature Khrushchevs. Nixon observed: "There was a steel-like quality, a cold determination, a tough amoral ruthlessness which somehow had been instilled into every one of them."[7]

Nixon's crusade was based on the moral judgment that communism is simply and savagely evil. His black and white dualism, expressed in the cold war, fanned the fires of belligerency on both sides. Nixon said that he would be willing to commit the country militarily against communism anywhere in the world. He was sure the United States would emerge victorious from "the greatest drama in human history."[8] Henderson observes: "What is missing in Nixon's politics and his religion is a consistent recognition of the tragic and demonic."[9] The closest Nixon seems

95

to have come to a perception of evil was in communism. Yet however evil Marxism may have been, committing horrible crimes, it is not responsible by itself for the human propensity to violence. This menace is thousands of years old. Henderson believes the irrationality, arrogance, and narcosis of Soviet Russia have been matched in kind if not in degree in the United States.

KISSINGER AND DÉTENTE

Secretary of State Kissinger has stood for a policy of détente. He became known personally by Jimmy Carter when he visited at the Governor's mansion in Atlanta. Bruce Mazlish, Kissinger's biographer, observes:

> Kissinger's life and work raise in passionate fashion some of the key problems of history in general and of our era in particular.[10]

They make clear that foreign policy cannot avoid questions of morality, power, and the meaning of history.

Kissinger came to the United States as a refugee during the holocaust. Of Jewish Orthodox background, he is not practicing, but did take part in the confirmation ceremony of the children of his first marriage. Kissinger does not share American optimism. His more pessimistic philosophy of life has a sense of the tragic and is conditioned by the memory of what happened to his own people under the Nazis. Yet in many respects, his intellectualism is more German than Jewish. Both roots led him to rejection of an uncritical nationalism as well as the idea of progress. Kissinger's great value to Nixon was that he had an overall view of foreign policy. His contempt for the president's lack of intellectual ability was well known among his advisors. At times, he spoke of our "meatball president." Mazlish argues: ''In the case of Richard Nixon there was no intellectualization, no conceptual system worthy of the name, that mediated between him and his psychological impulses.''[11] Mazlish believes he operated directly on the political process, deterred only by opportunism and his inner needs. He says, ''There was no Nixon policy; only a personality.''[12] The course of history gave the president almost unlimited power. ''Nixon showed that he had few limits, of conviction or intellectualization . . . Kissinger is quite different.''[13]

The Harvard professor's writings on diplomacy were already known before he came to the White House from Rockefeller's team. Nixon wished to negotiate the end of the war in Vietnam and used Kissinger as his agent. The president had bluffed in campaign rhetoric, claiming to know how to end hostilities. He now painfully strove to make good on this promise. Mazlish characterizes Kissinger as an active conservative who regards himself as a White Revolutionary, a conservative using the power of revolutionary acts, as it were, stealing their thunder. Carter's self-image is a different one; he seems to read them more positively. A number of commentators agree that Kissinger's long-range historical and strategic understanding is flawed by his conservative world view. They argue that Kissinger does not understand the new world of science and technology. Revolutionary political, social, or economic developments and aspiration do not arouse his sympathies. ''On the short range, tactical level, his skills are excellent.''[14] But his desire for stability causes him to make faulty analogies with earlier times.

While a soldier, Kissinger was greatly influenced by Fritz Kraemer, a German refugee of noble background and conservative Lutheran conviction. Kissinger found in this low-ranking officer a sense of what men should be fighting for. He also understood and accepted Kraemer's warning that love is not effective on the docks at Marseilles. Again and again, Kissinger emphasizes that politics is about power. The fact can hardly be denied, especially in international relations. To deal with it, Kissinger revived the balance of power theory against cold war fanaticism.

Kissinger has expressed justifiable contempt for attempts to solve international problems by friendship and good will alone. Kissinger singles out the strategy which Eisenhower and John Foster Dulles used on the Russians. Ideology, the anti-Communist crusade, are equally irrelevant. The problem is not just one of friendship but of stabilizing power.

POWER

Kissinger's own view is: "Power as an instrument in its own right has no fascination for me. . . . What interests me is what one can achieve with power. Splendid things, believe me."[15]

An elitist, Kissinger has given small priority to the American democratic tradition of checks and balances, believing that it can inhibit the efficacy of foreign policy. He speaks often about honor, prestige, and respectability with the goal of strength at home in the face of the enemy. He is not a moralist like Carter. His major commitment is to the use of power to insure the preservation of order and international stability, and he resists its direction toward novel or revolutionary aims. He has not been interested in a change of values or restoration of right ones either at home or abroad.

Underlying such policy is Kissinger's belief that American nuclear power has been rendered virtually powerless by the fear of retaliation. The president cannot change this situation at will, and Carter has spoken of the Second Coming of Christ. Whatever relevance such a religious eschatology of last things may have, it is clear the end of civilization could come in a nuclear holocaust. Man's own actions could obliterate human life on this planet almost completely. Faced by the possibility of such destruction, Nixon gave up his all-out attack on communism. An earlier black and white analysis, with its unrelenting struggle against evil, shaded into grays in détente. Kissinger's prognosis in such circumstances has been a kind of Bismarkian if not Machiavellian realism, not idealism. No doubt, Carter will try to change this.

Tad Szulc has written in the *New Republic:* "Reality imposes certain limitations on excessive innovation, and even on campaign rhetoric. In the end, then, much of Carter's foreign policy will depend on what he calls style and what, inevitably, will be the subtleties and nuances of practical policies."[16] The criticism is probably a sound one, that Kissinger makes not the slightest effort to see what Hegel understood.[17] Writing after the French Revolution, the German philosopher saw that Napoleon was not just a despotic adventurer but an embodiment of revolutionary ideals. This in spite of the fact that he had betrayed them. Kissinger views him as a tyrant. But this is not all that can be said about him.

CARTER'S POPULISM

Will Carter's openness be more successful than Kissinger's elitism and secrecy? Carter's acceptance speech, following his nomination, was described by *Time* magazine as a Populist sermon. Asked if he considered himself a Populist, Carter replied, "I think so."[18] The candidate spoke out against the "political and economic elite," the "big-shot crooks" who never go to jail and the "unholy, self-perpetuating alliances [that] have been formed between money and politics." In his inaugural address as governor in Georgia, he castigated the "powerful and privileged few'' and called for ''simple justice'' for ''the poor, rural, weak, or black.'' Populism has centered more on domestic issues than on foreign policy. There are some parallels with European socialism but it lacks class consciousness. Midwestern Populism inspired William Jennings Bryan's free-silver policy, designed to put more money into circulation. Populism's confusion of class is illustrated by Bryan's grouping together of workers, small business men, and farmers, policemen, barbers, secretaries, and school teachers; all but the idle rich may be included.[19] Occasionally, anti-capitalism is joined by a doctrine of opportunity calling for ''the poorest, the weakest, the humblest'' to have a fair chance. Such idealism does have implications for foreign policy.

Carter has said his strength comes directly from the populace. Any decisions he makes must be objective and fair—''to redress grievances and overcome the last vestiges of the consequences of . . . . . discrimination.'' In the future his ''support must come from the population as a whole.''

How does this conviction translate into international relations? As a youth, Carter read Tolstoy's *War and Peace* and was impressed with the way that history was made by the people more than by their superiors. It did not give him naiveté about human nature, but a larger view of history. Populism as a movement has been short lived in the United States. As a perennial theme in American politics, it has roots as far back as the revolution. Thomas Jefferson, the first Secretary of State, was its father. John Adams complained that the Declaration of Independence contained no new ideas, but was only a commonplace compilation. Jefferson replied that its object was not to find new principles or arguments never before thought of, or even merely to say what had been said before, but to be so plain and so firm as to command assent. In the same spirit, Jefferson opposed paternalistic justifications for authority.

The Populist doctrine of human nature is relatively optimistic although not necessarily naive. The Populist trusts the people and has faith in America. Unlike Marxism, Populism needs no revolution to end all revolutions. More important is restoration of power to the people. William Jennings Bryan expressed the Populist sentiment: ''What this country needs is not more brains but more heart.''[20] Professional conceptualizers become obsessed with research and theories, and consequently desensitized to moral issues. It is not enough to know how to orchestrate bombing attacks or to mechanize sex. More than academic and technological skills are needed.

CRITICISM

Carter's idealism has been attacked bluntly. For example, Charles Henderson writes: ''It is a sentimental illusion to believe that complex political problems can be solved by an appeal to compassion and love.''[21] The chief instrument of love, he argues, is persuasion, and justice will never be guaranteed by persuasion alone. James Burnham comments in the *National Review,* ''It is a primary theme of Carter's that government ought to be moral.''[22] The president speaks of honesty, integrity, fairness, liberty, justice, courage, patriotism, compassion, love! A government ought to exemplify these traits—to be as good as its people. Abroad as well as at home, American policy must be one of goodness, decency, compassion, idealism, and trust. Burnham's rejoinder is: ''In foreign policy the Carterian virtues are a manifest absurdity.'' If the United States really lives by them, ''it is going to be terribly lonely.'' Carter's terms are

101

not only highly charged emotionally; reference to them interferes with the prudent determination of public policy.

Part of the controversy turns about the theologian whom Carter cites most often, Reinhold Niebuhr. Niebuhr emphasizes that nations and governments are collective entities which differ in structure and essence from individuals. In their collective structures, they are subject to psychological impulses very different from those which motivate conduct on a personal level. Niebuhr understands ''the power of self-interest and collective egoism in all inter-group relations'' as belonging permanently to human beings and their circumstances. Collective behavior has a brutal character, disguised or open: the state must use coercion, in police power and warfare, in ways which are intolerable in personal relations. Burnham concludes that Carter's utopian, really Manichean, call for a politics of moral perfection will slip all too easily into a politics of crusades and fanaticism. He states: ''Probably Carter's government-is-love talk is only sentimentality plus demagogy. Reinhold Niebuhr would have hoped so.'' The question remains, however, whether Burnham has really read Niebuhr as well as Carter. All too easily, Niebuhr has been used to defend a kind of realism which he did not advocate.

PROSPECTS

Can Carter and his foreign policy advisors really displace the Kissinger legacy? Clearly, his intentions are not those of a White Revolutionary. Refusing elitism, he affirms the dignity and worth of the common man throughout the world. Can Carter carry his Populist dream world-wide, inspired by religious belief in the dignity of man? After his election, Carter commented he hoped to establish a national position, ''based not on military might or economic pressure of political persuasion but on the fact that we are right and decent.''[23] No doubt, Carter will meet hostility and disappointment as he attempts to implement this goal. Kucharsky, an evangelical commentator, warns about over-optimism concerning human nature. But, after all, institutional religion has too often been aligned with the old order of society, leaving revolution or reform to the more secularly minded.

Carter is not a utopian reformer, espousing the kind of self-righteous idealism Kissinger abhors. However, he is concerned for freedom and equality, and will use his influence and power on their behalf. He believes, like Kissinger, that foreign policy must have an over-all strategy; his is a different one. Nor is he just for plugging of dikes and opposing communism:

> I think there has been in Kissinger's foreign policy an inclination to divide the world into two major power blocs and almost force nations to take a stand: 'I'm for the U.S., I'm against the Soviet Union.' 'I'm for the Soviet Union. I'm against the U.S.'
> . . . what I'll do is try to get away from that position and deal with nations on an individual basis as far as what is best for their own people.[24]

So, Carter is not captured by cold war mythology; he knows that there is no alternative to détente. Simplistic judgments of good and evil all too easily miss what is going on. He must face problems both of atomic disarmament and world revolution. His long term goal will be to make justice more effective in an imperfect, selfish, and sinful world. Will Carter's more optimistic view of man be more successful than Kissinger's ''realism''? As Pat Cadell, Carter's aide, has written, ''Skill and luck—they're both key parts of the political process.''[25] It is worth a try. After all, what is realism?

7. *Playboy* and the Sermon on the Mount

THE INCIDENT

Playboy reporter Robert Scheer stood in the doorway of Jimmy Carter's home in Plains, Georgia, still carrying his tape recorder. He was about to end the last of a series of interviews which had started before Carter's nomination when the candidate had been seeking attention from every possible source. Scheer decided to ask a final question about the nominee's puritanical image. Carter was tired and could not shut either the door or his mouth, as a national magazine observed. He replied: "I've looked on a lot of women with lust. I've committed adultery in my heart many times."[1] Carter explained this does not mean he condemns someone who not only looks on a woman with lust but leaving his own wife, commits adultery. Christ says, don't consider yourself better than someone else because one person commits adultery with many women while the other is loyal to his wife. Carter used two off-color, slang words in expressing these thoughts on adultery.

Scheer is supposed to have thought, "For the first time,

I'm getting the real Carter. He finally expressed himself in a way readers could respond to.'' Carter's remarks were the most misunderstood and explosive of the entire campaign. On his own admission, he was indiscreet. He apologized to the public early in the second debate with President Ford.

Newsweek magazine attempted to credit Carter with a complex triple play: he was trying to explain his beliefs, to reassure people that he was not sitting in judgment, and to build a linguistic bridge to the *Playboy* constituency.[2] It came out in newspaper headlines otherwise: ''Sex, Sin, Temptation—Carter's Candid Views.'' ''On Sin and Lust: I'm Human. . . . I'm Tempted.'' Doris Kearns, a writer who interviewed Carter for magazine profiles, reports: ''He said just about the same thing he did to *Playboy*.''[3] Carter said that while everyone talks about extramarital relations and adultery, the most important thing is to conquer lust.

A good Sunday School lesson! Commented *Newsweek:* this was sound enough doctrine, an honest reflection of Carter's thoughts, ''but politically speaking the message just wasn't getting across.''

What Carter said evoked endless humor. He appeared in a cartoon looking with lust at a sensuous, nude Statue of Liberty. There were descriptions of how the president would feel when introduced to attractively dressed women at White House receptions. Carter's fidelity in his own marriage was reaffirmed by his wife in necessary campaign rhetoric; it was not in question.

Actually, his remarks were given to illustrate how Christ's demands in the Sermon on the Mount increase rather than decrease the imperative of love—not just for worthy and righteous behavior but for purity of heart! Was this understood? *Time* magazine, for example, tried them out on a bakery operator from Freemont, California, Robert Bailey, who said in reply: ''I'm a Baptist myself and for a Bible-totin' Baptist to say those things—well, they were crude.''[4] Bailey did not see why Carter had to make a national confession, revealing all his deep inner thoughts. One does not become a great man in this way.

PRIDE AND HUMILITY

Carter was in part echoing his favorite theologian, Reinhold Niebuhr, who speaks of pride rather than sensuality as the root of sin. What Niebuhr calls the impossible possibilities of Christian love probe beyond action to intent. Jesus' beatitudes do not give a perfect blueprint for an ideal society. Rather, they express the will of God, identifying the perfection that exists in God's kingdom. Evil is traced back to its source in motivation. God's judgment evokes repentance and in the end, salvation and blessedness. Carter did not gloss over or deny the presence of mixed motives among Christians. His position was psychologically sound; he did not disparage the body.

Dean William Wolf of the Episcopal Divinity School in Cambridge, Massachusetts said: ''It sounds to me like good theology and good honest human experience brought together.''[5] Carter's own pastor in Plains said, ''I have no particular objection to it . . . but I would have used other words to describe the same thing.''[6] The effect was positive on Father Andrew Greeley who earlier had been outspoken against the Carter candidacy. Greeley changed his mind about the man. He is now convinced that Carter is human, not rigidly self-righteous. Mr. Carter's talk of lust may ''sound to us terribly dirty,'' he explained to the Catholic readers in his column, but noted that it could be translated into their rhetoric by the much more clinical phrasing, ''I was tempted.''[7]

Christianity teaches not only the essential goodness of creation, but the sinfulness of man. Carter had grasped the central claim of Christianity for love of God and the neighbor. Often Jesus warned against the attitude of the publican: self-righteousness, lack of humility and sense of need for forgiveness.

So the candidate told his interviewer: what Christ taught about most was pride. One person should not think of himself as any better than anybody else. Carter recounted Christ's vivid story about two people who went into a church. It is a parable, of course. One was a Pharisee, an official of the church and he said, "Lord, I thank you I'm not like all those other people." He kept all of the Commandments and gave a tenth of everything in a tithe. He prayed, "I'm here to give thanks for making me more acceptable in your sight." The other man, despised by the nation, went into the place, and prostrating himself on the floor said, "Lord, have mercy on me a sinner. I'm not worthy to lift my eyes to heaven." Christ asked the disciples which one of the two had justified his life. Of course, it was obviously the one who was humble.

While accepting the Christian imperative for purity of motive and intent, Carter recognizes the continuing presence of sin in the life of the believer. Sanctification is not complete.

"I try not to commit a deliberate sin," he said. Yet Carter recognizes that he is going to do it, anyhow. He knows that he is human and he's tempted. "And Christ set some almost impossible standards for us."

But does this not lead to overconfession as is clear from Carter's comment on lust and his acknowledgment that it persists in his own life? Carter emphasized, "Christ said, 'I tell you that anyone who looks on a woman with lust in his heart already committed adultery.' " As Martin Marty of the University of Chicago points out, if he had said, "Jesus' standards are very high. Jesus said, 'Whoever hateth his brother is a murderer, I have killed people.' '' There would not have been a word of criticism. Hating isn't such a big deal.[8]

THE KINGDOM OF GOD

William Miller of Indiana University pointed out, in an article, ''Candor and Naiveté—Defending Carter's Heresies,'' that Carter gave an informed exposition of the best sub-part of the Christian doctrine—the part about forgiveness and humility.[9] His heresy was not against Christian orthodoxy but prideful moralism. The drastic character of Jesus' love ethic appears in the so-called hard sayings. In fact, Carter cites one of them, the man who lusts or hates has already committed adultery or murder in the heart. Other such precepts are assembled in the Sermon on the Mount: swear not, resist not evil doers. Jesus also enjoins childlike trust in God. ''Consider the lilies of the field,'' he said, ''they toil not neither do they spin. Yet Solomon in all his glory was not arrayed as one of these.'' Such sayings are not prudential models for earthly society by which a president might govern. They derive from and are a prescription for the ''kingdom of God.''

The kingdom, God's perfect rule of justice and righteousness, is not yet triumphant, although Jesus enjoins men to pray for its coming. Wickedness has not been destroyed fully; the struggle between good and evil goes on. According to the New Testament, the kingdom of God is not something men can bring to pass or build; at most, they can only prepare for it by repentance and faith. Although Jesus' teachings are highly internalized, the kingdom of God is more than an inner state. Christians are enjoined to respond to God's mercy and love even in the present imperfect society. They are to accept other persons not for their merits

109

but because God loves them—even sinners. Carter attempts to make what Christian ethicists call "a leap to the side of the neighbor,"—loving him and identifying with him. On prudential terms, such strategy is nonsensical. It is not calculating. The motivation is religious, love of neighbor out of gratitude to God for His encompassing love.

Professor Miller observes that reading the text of the *Playboy* interview gave him an entirely different impression from the sprinkled snippets in the news, not to mention "all the leering and wailing and scolding" that followed its release. Miller found the effect to be so different in fact as to make him angry at the distortions which the world of high powered publicity has imposed. Theology, simple or complex, is not understood there. Miller finds the review remarkably forthright—a candid performance. Carter was asked everything and answered everything, allowing himself to be more vulnerable than most politicians ever do. As informed an exposition as has been offered from any American politician got turned clear around and made into something offensive to those people who should have been most deeply impressed with it.

The interviewers kept badgering Carter from *Playboy*'s home territory, expressing fear of what a religious man would say, do, or imply on the subject of sex to "make us feel guilty." Carter, like an earnest Sunday School teacher, in preaching style attempted to persuade his interviewers that he would not be a self-righteous, censorious president. Miller observes that two of the most religiously literate presidents, Theodore Roosevelt and Woodrow Wilson, emphasized the righteous, law-giving side of biblical religion. Carter by contrast gave priority to humility and the finiteness of those who believe in God. It would be "sinful" to claim absolute finality for one's own point of view or goodness, he explained.

JUSTIFICATION BY FAITH

Carter applied Jesus' hard saying to himself, trying to make his point to "those uncomprehending secular folk." No person can fulfill so high a demand, to live without lust "in the heart." The Sermon on the Mount raises the standard to the level of the impossible and Christians are cast back into contrition and non-judgmental forgiveness toward others. Salvation cannot be by good works but only from God's forgiveness and grace. This was the point Carter was making, not really anything about lust. Miller describes Carter as trying with winsome naiveté to explain to these unlikely prospects for conversion the heart of the Christian doctrine of justification by faith—in Luther, in Augustine, in Paul, in Jesus himself.

Miller observes that many of Carter's readers never seem to have heard of or read the fifth chapter of Matthew. Yet one would be hard pressed to find a piece of writing of comparable length more fundamental to the history of the West than the Sermon on the Mount. For Carter, there turned out to be grave political risks in citing a passage so unknown to many of his audience. More than this, he lost votes among the pious who seemed to believe as well that Carter had gratuitously volunteered some comments about his lustfulness. Columnists and reporters whose own fornication and adultery had been gossiped in Washington were shocked by proxy for what they believed moralists would say all over America. Miller concludes that the worldly-wise faulted Carter not for sin, which they do not believe in, but for making a mistake, which act in their eyes is far worse.[10] It was not a question of moral integrity. He just had not been prudent, calculating, smart in his own self-interest. The cynical urban world that created *Playboy* magazine and keeps it going and shares its vulgar world view criticized Carter for answering the questions of its own interviewers with full openness. Such is the peril which an honest man faces in the not-so-honest world because of his own honesty.

The New Testament is not concerned primarily with lust, but with love. Through Christ's death and resurrection love is available to all men, great and small, young and old, male and female. Like other Christians, Carter knows that such love has never been realized fully in society; it can never be attained perfectly on earth. Christian belief in the final triumph of righteousness is not affirmed on prudential grounds. Often amid tragic circumstances, there is no easy answer apart from sacrifice. A political leader who promised to live up to the ideal of love unequivocally would be irresponsible and utopian. Carter commented: ''The thing that's drummed into us all the time is not to be proud, not to be better than anyone else.'' Christians should not look down on people but strive to make themselves acceptable in God's eyes. The simple truth that men must be saved by grace should be recognized. ''It's just a free gift through faith in Christ. This gives us a mechanism by which we can relate permanently to God.'' Carter will not speak for other persons. But he claims for himself a sense of peace, equanimity, and assurance from this source.

LIVING ''BETWEEN THE TIMES''

Christians like Carter who take Jesus' claims seriously must live between the times. God's kingdom and righteousness have been revealed in the coming of Jesus. However, the final culmination of history when evil will be destroyed by God's power has not yet come. Jesus' teachings are to be obeyed in preparation for the coming of the kingdom. Albert Schweitzer's epoch-making book, *The Quest of the Historical Jesus,* made clear for all subsequent New Testament scholarship that Jesus' teachings have an "eschatological" setting.[11] Eschatology means last things, death and resurrection, the last judgment and the end of the world. The outlook is clearly evident throughout the Gospels. To attempt to remove it from the New Testament record as Thomas Jefferson did in his abridgement of the Gospels compromises the Christian doctrine of sin. Jefferson, in fact, cast Jesus in the model of an Enlightenment philosopher who would have been at home in Monticello.

Historically, Jesus' roots were in the Hebrew prophetic tradition with its expectation of the imminent coming of the kingdom of God. He believed that the struggle between good and evil would not remain forever unresolved, but that only the Father knew the exact day and hour of the end. Both Jews and Christians live in a world which is often characterized by injustice, oppression, and violence. As believers in God, they affirm that there is something which is more than the apparently senseless facts of life. The God of the Bible is both just and loving. Individually, he commands love for persons. He also demands justice of both nations and their rulers. Although the love of God is evident in the Old Testament record, Christians believe that it has been revealed definitively in the life, death, and Resurrection of Jesus Christ. God's love becomes concrete and available in Christ as the mediator between God and man.

SIN

Does man need to be redeemed? Is sin a meaningful category as Carter believes? Reinhold Niebuhr, who has been cited for his influence on Carter, has attempted to give modern relevance to the Christian understanding of evil.

Niebuhr asks how Jesus' "love universalism and love per-fectionism" are to be understood today. According to Niebuhr, Jesus' love-ethic goes beyond the bounds set by natural human impulse. Christianity is a religion with an ethic so pure that it has difficulty in coming to terms with political realities. The profoundest versions of Christianity have not believed that the cross could make sacrificial love simply into historical success. Niebuhr's way of warning against such superficiality is to say that the law of love is a law and not yet a law. He describes it as a norm but not an obligation. What he means is that love is not a simple possibility, since man's freedom has been corrupted by sin. Full perfection is not attainable in history.

Men dream of an ideal world in which property, govern-ment, nationality, and ethical distinctions will all disap-pear. When this does not come to pass, cynicism sets in.

> Einstein once believed that if he could get two per cent of the population to disavow war he might succeed in abolishing it. How deeply ironic that this very man would have been the one to write the letter of introduction to President Roosevelt for a group of physicists, whose visit to the President initiated the whole process that finally gave us the hydrogen bomb.[12]

Rational man and his age stumbles upon and becomes involved in the perennial problem of sin and guilt. Reason alone is no answer. Neither science nor political power brings escape from the hopes, fears, ambitions and anx-ieties of individual or national experience. The source of evil is self-love, sin, not just residual natural impulses. Niebuhr attacks as illusory the claim that the Christian idea of the sinfulness of man is outmoded.

DRASTIC LOVE

Jesus' teachings are more internally probing, concerned with motive and intent, than those of Confucius or Mohammed. Unlike them, he offered no explicit political program. For this reason, it is often said that Christianity is personal and beyond politics. "Blessed are the pure in heart, for they shall see God," said Jesus. As Kierkegaard observed in commentary on this text, anything less than purity of heart is sin. But love and purity of motive are not always effective; indeed they have been crucified in history. What is the role of love? The difference between prudential and self-denying ultimate "eschatological" love is not always clear in Carter's pronouncements. Not the terminology, but the real difference may yet return to plague him! Jesus commands that His followers be reconciled with the brother, that they forgive seventy times seven. Is this possible in politics? Does it not preclude tough practical decisions? Carter is not hypocritical or insincere in his affirmation of Christian love. Yet the text, "Render unto Caesar that which is Caesar's and to God that which is God's," must remain for him. Carter is Caesar, a democratic president, but holding political power. He cannot hold office on the basis of love alone.

Christians dare not disavow their responsibility for justice in world affairs if their faith is to be more than a superficial moralism. Yet they must find a way to bring the love ethic to bear on their political decisions. Everyone knows that as president, Carter will be forced to make calculated and discriminate judgments between conflicting claims. At the same time, Carter seems to agree with Niebuhr's remark that there is no human situation in which love does not present possibilities of action higher than the

115

conventional and traditional customs and habits of men. This is part of the meaning of the Sermon on the Mount. Systems of justice cannot maintain themselves without inspiration from a deeper dimension in the purifying effect of sacrificial love. At this point, one touches the fundamental Christian understanding of the relation between love and justice. Christian faith is not just a moralism. Love does not abrogate justice but fulfills and completes it.

UTOPIAN OR REALISTIC?

Too easily, utopian claims are made for good intentions. It is much more difficult for societies or nations to love in the same way as persons. In fact, it is dubious whether they can do so. This is one of the reasons why Carter speaks of justice rather than love in international relations. Will Carter be an unbending moralist as president? In his *Playboy* interview he attempted to say no. He knows with Niebuhr that careful and discriminating judgments concerning competing rights and interests must be made. He does not affirm love alone, but seeks for justice in a sinful world. As a political activist, he has had to work on the problem for himself. A critic might say that his Southern Baptist background has taught him more about individual conversion than Christian social ethics. But this may not turn out to be true. He should not be expected to move from theory alone any more than a creative artist works by art criticism or an inventive, discovering scientist from philosophy of science. To be really meaningful, Christian ethics must develop in situations. Carter is willing, indeed he feels a duty to apply their norms personally and existentially. What he attempts may work more readily than the cynics expect. The alternatives are chaos and hatred.

8. Evangelicals

IS CARTER AN EVANGELICAL?

The president is often described as an evangelical Christian but not a fundamentalist. *Time* magazine quoted him as saying, "I find it difficult to question Holy Scripture, but I admit I do have trouble with Paul sometimes, especially when he says that a woman's place is with her husband, and that she should keep quiet and should cover her head in church. I just can't go along with him on that."[1]

Carter was asked: "You've been described as a fundamental Baptist. That means you take everything in the Bible quite literally. Possibly you believe that the whale swallowed Jonah. Is that a fair characterization?"

Carter replied, "I don't believe everything in the Bible to be literally true. I don't think the earth was created in seven days as we know days now and I reserve the right to make my own interpretation."[2]

The Greek word, "evangel," means good news. How has it come to be applied to a particular party of Christians? Richard Quebedeaux in his book, *The Young Evangelicals,* traces the term from the period of the Reformation. He reports that contemporary evangelicalism is "by no means unified in the fine points (and even some of the not-so-fine points) of doctrine.'' As a party, it affirms three major theological principles: (1) the complete reliability and final authority of the Bible in matters of faith and practice, (2) personal faith in Jesus Christ as Savior from sin, (3) the urgency of seeking to convert others to him as Lord. Quebedeaux defines the term experientially as: ''Knowing Christ, like knowing any person on a deep level, is an experience.''[3] Evangelicals view the new birth as the beginning of this growing experience.

Quebedeaux judges that there are at least thirty-three million church-going evangelicals in America today. This type of reckoning led the Roman Catholic, Michael Novak, to exclaim: ''There is a hidden religious power base in American culture which our secular biases prevent many of us from noticing. Jimmy Carter has found it.''[4] The power of evangelicals is easily overstated in an election year. One can identify common attitudes, but there is no unanimous agreement even on the meaning of the Bible. Evangelicals represent a kind of conservative, low-church piety which has not gone the way of modernism, culture conformity, or optimism about man and history. Often, they have been described as outsiders.

FUNDAMENTALIST?

The Southern Baptists dominate in large regions of the South and Southwest and are not outsiders. At times they have been called fundamentalists, evangelicals, pietists, and sectarians. The first two labels easily become too omnibus.

Holifield comments: ''The fundamentalists were strong in the Southern Baptist Convention in the 1920's, but within two decades their excesses sparked a backlash among religious conservatives.''[5] The latter were more preoccupied with interior piety than with doctrinal purity. Holifield notes that both the president's social commitments and his empiricism distinguish his religious faith from classical fundamentalism. He once referred to Paul Tillich as "a great theologian who is a little too liberal for a Baptist fundamentalist like me."[6] Then, he affirmed Tillich's conclusion that "when we quit searching and think we know the answers . . . perhaps at that moment we lose part of our religion." Such statements lead Holifield to say bluntly, "He is not a fundamentalist."

Sociologically, the Southern Baptists occupy a middle position between the more liberal Methodists, Presbyterians, and Episcopalians, on the one hand, and the Pentecostal and more radical separatist fundamentalist groups on the other.

In spite of their congregational piety, they are well organized. As the mainline church in the region, Southern Baptists have gone their own way. A certain kind of unbrotherly feeling about them has been summarized pointedly by Albert Outler of Southern Methodist University: "The fact is that Southern Baptists have been culturally isolated and are theologically unsophisticated."[7]

Outler alleges that they are without experience in dealing with evangelicals different from themselves. They lack any reference for working with Catholics, Jews, or secular moralists. The latter are regarded as unregenerated worldlings heading for damnation unless they are converted. Disparagingly, Outler charges that the Southern Baptists want a society ruled by leaders who know what the Word of God is. "The technical name for that is 'theocracy,' and their Napoleon, whether he likes it or not, is Jimmy Carter." Many Southern Baptists would contend that such an inclusive statement is unfair and does not recognize the wide diversity in their membership.

Before the Civil War, indeed throughout the nineteenth

century, the country was in the vast majority Protestant. In fact, the dominant pattern of religion could be called evangelical. It was low-church, non-liturgical, revivalist, and biblicist. This mode of religion re-established popular piety in America after the Revolutionary War. A revivalist piety of the heart, more than argument, kept the working classes from being lost to the churches in the United States as they were in Europe. Protest and reform went into low church sectarian piety rather than socialism or communism. Controversy about social action and the higher criticism of the Bible had not yet developed.

PUBLIC VERSUS PRIVATE PROTESTANTISM

Martin Marty of the University of Chicago speaks of an antithesis between Public Protestantism and Private Protestantism in the last century.[8] The former championed the American dream of progress and manifest destiny, optimistically affirming Christian influence in society through democracy. The freeing of the slaves was often cited as an example of Christian idealism, to be sure more acceptable in the North than in the South.

Protestant private piety was more conformist socially, emphasizing personal salvation over social change. Evangelist D. L. Moody, in the last century, and Billy Graham in the present, belong primarily to this tradition. Both have emphasized that man's greatest hope is the Second Coming of Christ and not any alleged growth of goodness in history.

Such a doctrine puts a very severe limit on Christian political action. To be sure, Graham has insisted on an end of racial discrimination, refusing segregated crusades. However, he did not join the protest against the war in Vietnam. Graham has been criticized for too close association with Richard Nixon, and he himself seems to recognize he was used. Graham said, following Nixon's bombing of Hanoi in December, 1972:

> I am convinced that God has called me to be a New Testament evangelist, not an Old Testament prophet! While some may interpret an evangelist to be primarily a social reformer or political activist, I do not! An evangelist is a proclaimer of the message of God's love and grace in Jesus Christ and the necessity of repentance and faith. . . . The people of the world need a new birth that only Christ can bring.[9]

John Coleman Bennett of Union Seminary, where Niebuhr taught, has commented:

> His eschatology enables him to chastise America without disturbing the particular *respectable* forms of power in our midst, especially those responsible for the use of power by our nation abroad.[10]

Yet Graham's campaigns have engendered social concern. Carter's first interracial experience after returning to Plains was in such a campaign.

Quebedeaux remarks, "Evangelicalism, as we have mentioned, repudiated the distasteful cultural and social elements of fundamentalism."[11] Evangelicals now shy away from the word "fundamentalism." The designation dates from the early twentieth century. Fundamentalism was defensive against modernism, evolution, and higher criticism of the Bible. Carter, when asked by Garry Wills about one of the most recent modes of the last, Biblical Form Criticism, replied with a question, "What is it?"[12] But he would know fundamentalism! Fundamentalism went beyond orthodox Christian doctrine in its literalism.

The program of this movement was spelled out in a series of ten small books, *The Fundamentals: A Testimony to the Truth*.[13] The name dates from these books and was not used earlier. They were published in 1910 under the sponsorship of two wealthy Los Angeles laymen, Milton and Lyman Stewart, associated with the Bible Institute movement. The ''five fundamentals of the faith'' were identified as (1) the verbal inspiration of the Bible, (2) the virgin birth of Christ, (3) His substitutionary atonement, (4) His bodily resurrection, and (5) His imminent and visible Second Coming.

There were periods between the two world wars when the fundamentalists could have captured a number of the mainline American churches. This did not come to pass, as their Biblical literalism together with their individualism went too far for the mainline church leadership.

Fundamentalists lost influence in society in their contest with modern science about evolution. William Jennings Bryan was the last great national spokesman for this view among politicians. Like Carter, he was a Populist, but a Methodist rather than a Baptist.

Bryan is remembered for his role in the Stokes Trial when he prosecuted a public school teacher who had dared to teach biological evolution openly in the classroom. His opponent was the famous criminal lawyer, Clarence Darrow. Bryan won the battle but lost the war! In the era, a whole generation of churchmen and scientists carried on the clash with intense feeling. The controversy now belongs largely to the past.

Like Carter, evangelicals no longer insist that the world came into existence in six days literally. Equally important, it is clear that evolution does not carry over into man's moral life and politics. An authentic piety, a Christian common sense has outlasted the controversy. Believers and unbelievers recognize that the ultimate issues of life and death are not answered by science alone. More important than stories about the beginning of life or the end of the world, is personal faith and love of God.

NEO-ORTHODOXY

The evangelicals' emphasis on grace and conversion is clearly biblical. Denominations like the Southern Baptists have preserved a sense of sin and forgiveness more than many so-called liberal groups. Theologically, the so-called Neo-Orthodoxy of Karl Barth, Paul Tillich, and the Niebuhrs, has long since replaced liberalism in most seminaries.

Some evangelicals see truth in some of the Neo-Orthodox emphases. They also see weaknesses in Neo-Orthodoxy. This mixed reaction is sensed by Quebedeaux who comments as an evangelical: "In Neo-Orthodoxy, there seemed to be no *real requirement* that a man repent and believe the Gospel."[14] A prophetic call for the creation of a just and equitable society tended to take the place of the traditional proclamation that all men and women are sinners. Encounter with Christ tended to become a vague and vacuous religious experience.

The Southern Baptist emphasis continued to be on the new birth, but in an often segregated church. Except for opposition to drinking and gambling, there has been limited social concern in many of the congregations. In all fairness, it should be noted that there is a growing interest in social responsibility among younger leaders. It is true, however, that Southern Baptists are more related to the status quo than Northern Evangelicals.

Attempts to classify Southern Baptists with Northern Evangelicals has brought a strong response from persons like Foy Valentine, Director of the Southern Baptist Convention Christian Life Commission: "We are *not* evangelicals. That's a Yankee word. They want to claim us because we are big and successful and growing every year."[15]

123

Valentine insists that Southern Baptists have their own traditions, hymns—and more students in their seminaries than all the Northern Evangelicals put together. ''We don't share their politics or their fussy fundamentalism, and we don't want to get involved in their theological witch hunts.''

DISPENSATIONALISM

Quebedeaux describes four contemporary parties: Separatist fundamentalism, open fundamentalism, establishment evangelicalism, and open evangelicalism. Separatist fundamentalism is led by Bob Jones University in South Carolina, Billy James Hargis in the Southwest and Carl McIntire in the East.

Dispensationalism gives separatist fundamentalism an extremely pessimistic view of the present world situation. It divides history into a number of successive periods or dispensations—innocence, conscience, promise, law, and grace. In each and every one, mankind is a failure. Its persistent wickedness will be doubly clear in the agony of the end time: (1) The rapture of the Church (its being lifted into the skies and then to heaven) will be followed in succession by (2) the seven-year Great Tribulation during the reign of the Anti-Christ, (3) the battle of Armageddon, (4) the thousand year millenial rule of Christ on earth, (5) Satan's rule over the world during a brief time of trouble, (6) the judgment of the Great White Throne. At last the Devil and his hosts will be thrown into a lake of everlasting fire. The saved will be taken to heaven.

Open fundamentalism is less extremely separatist. Hal Lindsey, a graduate of Dallas Theological Seminary, whose book, *The Late Great Planet Earth,* has been a best seller represents this view as does his seminary.

Quebedeaux does not wish to classify Billy Graham as a fundamentalist but as an establishment evangelical. However, Graham is a premillenialist. Quebedeaux's fourth party, to which he himself belongs, the new evangelicalism, has a marked aversion to Dispensationalism and its inherent apocalyptic speculations. It displays a fresh interest in the social dimension of the Gospel. It also emphasizes the necessity of meaningful sanctification following regeneration, the new birth. Quebedeaux belongs to this party which he says has begun to converse with representatives of other traditions.

Today, these divisions reappear in controversy over the literal interpretation of scripture. Southern Baptists like President McCall and Valentine do not want to become involved in the dispute. Harold Lindsell, an editor of the magazine, *Christianity Today,* has published a new book, *The Battle Over the Bible.*[16] Lindsell attacks one of the most successful evangelical seminaries, named for Charles E. Fuller, in Pasadena, California. He charges it has not been rigorous enough in affirmation of the verbal inspiration and inerrancy of the Bible.

At the other pole, one can identify evangelicals who wish to become involved in the problems of social reform. Such persons are increasingly concerned for responsible change, not just the preservation of the status quo. The Chicago Declaration of 1973 by Evangelicals for Social Action and the monthly magazine, *Sojourners,* embody this tradition.

President Carter is by background a conservative Christian who takes seriously repentance and faith as well as the need for humility. But he is not just a private Christian who has turned inward to piety alone and waits for the end of the world. On the contrary, he has been inspired to activism by Christian idealism and love. Concern for personal salvation, important for him, does not keep him back from witness in the world. His religion is not a defense against modernity.

125

CARTER'S IDENTITY

The question of Carter's identification as an evangelical is not as simple as it first appears to be. If the term is used to identify a simply emotional pietism, it cannot be applied to the president's religion. This is made clear in David Kucharsky's *The Man from Plains, The Mind and Spirit of Jimmy Carter.*[17] Kucharsky is managing editor of *Christianity Today,* a magazine associated with Billy Graham. Within this circle, a theology of social concern has been developed by such spokesmen as Latent Ford, Carl Henry, and Sherwood Wirt. Carter's major contact seems to have been most of all with his own denomination's program of mission and conversion. His visitations in Northern cities related his personal piety to the need for social justice.

The term "evangelical" comes closer to defining Carter's position than others. Reference to the political theories developed in Neo-Orthodoxy alone, does not explain his political participation. Carter has never adopted its drastic view of the all-pervasiveness and inevitability of sin.[18] Had he done so, he would be a different type of political activist. Reinhold Niebuhr, for example, repeatedly criticizes the sectarian and Baptist traditions.[19] His all-inclusive doctrine of original sin has not been emphasized by Carter. Niebuhr, in fact, underestimates the contribution of the free churches.

The president distinguishes between love and justice, institutional and individual strategies. But for him, the hope of making Christian love relevant and effective remains a present possibility. He believes that men need to be motivated away from selfishness toward love of neighbor. Institutions can be controlled and modified. It is the new birth which brings ethical sensitivity. Carter the evangelical has never accepted or perhaps even understood the "depths of despair'' in Neo-Orthodoxy. His sense of sin is acute, but he has also experienced conversion.

The sociologist, David Moberg, identifies a contemporary polarity in his book entitled, *Reversal, Evangelism Versus Social Concern.*[20] Before the Social Gospel movement and the Fundamentalist-Modernist debate, he observes, social concern and evangelism went hand in hand. Such was the case, for example, in leading evangelists of the past: Charles G. Finney, Charles H. Spurgeon, and T. de Witt Talmadge.

But with the rise of the Social Gospel and the Modernist-Fundamentalist controversy, an evident polarization took place within American Protestantism. Evangelism became personal evangelism alone. Social concerns were neglected. Moberg calls this the ''Great Reversal.'' He urges that the Great Reversal must be reversed! Christians ought no longer to remain divided between activists who crusade against entrenched social evils and pietists who emphasize only the life of prayer, worship, devotion, and personal evangelism.

Moberg argues against the division in principle, believing that these perspectives are both intrinsic to the Christian life. Indeed they are interdependent. Pietism is the root and activism the fruit. It may be that this Great Reversal is already being righted, knowingly or unknowingly, in persons like President Carter.

9. Other Believers— Roman Catholics and Jews

CARTER'S RELATION TO ROMAN CATHOLICISM

Jimmy Carter, the Baptist Christian, lives in a pluralistic society. Roman Catholic and Jewish votes are necessary to win a presidential election. In Carter's study at Plains, Georgia, are busts of two earlier chief executives: Abraham Lincoln, who was not a church member, and John Fitzgerald Kennedy, the first Roman Catholic president of the United States.[1] The Carter family admired the Kennedys long before Jimmy had any plans for the presidency. John F. Kennedy was of Irish descent. Some of Carter's Protestant ancestors lived in Ireland before the coming of the Kennedys. While these two parties of Christians live with tolerance in the American environment, religious hostility continues in their earlier home country even to the present.

Carter's South is still a largely Protestant region. Its cities have remained Protestant while Boston, New York, and Chicago have elected Catholic mayors. The president's own exposure to Roman Catholic worship and theology does not appear to have been very great. In the past, Southern Baptists have not given much attention to interconfessional dialogue. Indeed, they have often withdrawn from it. Some of Carter's Spanish speaking converts in his missionary work in the North were probably nominally Roman Catholic. Less than a decade later, during the election campaign, he called on Cardinal Cooke in New York City and attended mass while campaigning among Poles in Chicago.

President Kennedy had to reckon with the fact that one quarter of the nation's church membership is Baptist. Carter cannot ignore the fact that as much as one third is Roman Catholic by baptism. Comparisons are complicated by the fact that the Roman Catholic Church, unlike Baptists, begins counting members from infancy. Carter knows that the United States is no longer a simply Protestant nation as in the earlier part of the last century. It is made up of three socially accepted groups, Protestant, Roman Catholic, and Jewish. A creative national life together requires good faith and recognition of sincerity on the part of each. There is nothing in Carter's background as governor to suggest that he will discriminate confessionally or make Baptist appointments as President.

Carter dispatched a carefully written letter to the International Eucharistic Congress which met in Philadelphia during August of 1976. He wrote:

> Be assured that my family and I are with you in spirit.
>
> The international congress reaffirming God's love for all men seems especially appropriate at a time when churches of all denominations are threatened by overt oppression, by apathy or by despair born of social injustice. . . .
>
> May this congress remind all Americans of all faiths of the outstanding role that Catholics have played in the founding, preservation, and prospering of the republic, and may this Eucharistic Congress serve to lift up the hearts of believers

throughout the world, as it reaffirms our sense of brotherhood, at a time when faith and spirituality are gravely threatened over vast areas of this planet.[2]

During the election campaign, Carter met with Roman Catholic bishops to talk about the question of abortion. At the conclusion of their discussion, he said, characteristically, "I will not ask for your prayers that I win, but I will ask your prayers that I do the right thing."[3]

ISSUES

Some Roman Catholics as well as Protestants believe that it is unfortunate that the question of abortion was raised during the election campaign. In the end, Carter was able to ignore it in his speeches. Roman Catholic opinion recognized that there were other issues of importance as well. As Carter implied, to convince persons that abortion is morally wrong is different from legislating on it. The complexity of the issue is all too easily obscured in the heat of a campaign. A Roman Catholic layman, William V. Shannon of *The New York Times* has observed:

> The risk is that the church by concentrating public attention so intensively on the abortion problem may be perceived as a single issue constituency.[4]

Instead, it should bear witness to the Christian message on a wide range of human concerns. Shannon warns that the church should not allow itself to be downgraded as a special interest group. It is not comparable with the gun lobby or the textile manufacturers looking for import quota support.

Father Robert Drinan, a Jesuit priest and member of the House of Representatives from the fourth district in Massachusetts, endorsed Carter before the election. The rea-

131

sons which he gave, writing in the magazine of his order, *America,* were based on ''Carter's commitment to Christian concerns.''[5] Father Drinan argued the case for similarity with the social teachings of the Roman Catholic Church, focusing on the issues of arms control, concern for the third world, and domestic social problems. Drinan wondered whether upper middle-income Catholics were not increasingly using issues like abortion to cover up the fundamental lesson of the papal social encyclicals and the Second Vatican Council: ''A just and compassionate government must make real sacrifices to extend true equality to its poor as well as its powerful.'' Carter did receive the majority of Roman Catholic votes, but not by as large a margin as Kennedy, Johnson, or Humphrey.

Southern Baptists as well as Roman Catholics have had their own kind of separatism. Yet they have not known the deep hostility to the Counter Reformation which has persisted in Europe. Of course, Baptist prejudice against the Roman Catholic Church has not disappeared fully. Mutual defensiveness and intolerance persist on both sides. However, the pattern is unlike that of some countries in Europe where division among Christians had been so deep that only in concentration camps, during the Second World War, did they really come to know each other. Today, Protestants and Roman Catholics increasingly recognize common threats and opportunities as Carter indicated in his letter to the Eucharistic Congress.

POPE JOHN AND PRESIDENT KENNEDY

In fact, there are at least two chasms to bridge. The first is the longstanding one from the Reformation and Counter Reformation which lives on in violence in Northern Ireland today. The second is the cultural distance between American Roman Catholics—from other parts of the country—and Southern Baptists. Differences are sociological and psychological, not simply theological.

A variety of factors contributed to improved relations following the Second World War: a new ecumenical openness dates from the Second Vatican Council which Pope John XXIII convened. Baptists note in particular the official acceptance of tolerance and freedom of conscience by the Council. Its meeting—in many respects quite unexpected in the normal course of events—reflected the openness and love evident in Pope John's person. In America, John F. Kennedy broke through barriers of prejudice and bigotry to attain the highest office in the land. Affirming the separation of church and state, he drew significant Southern Baptist support for his stand against government subsidy to parochial schools. Before his assassination, Kennedy had won the love and admiration of Protestants and Jews as well as his own co-religionists. Americans of all faiths mourned his death and honored his contribution. It would have been politically dangerous, probably suicidal, for Kennedy to talk as much about religion as Carter has done. Although Irish in background, Kennedy had a Harvard University education. His image was more that of a secular idealist than a Roman Catholic protagonist.

Although he observed the duties of piety in his own community, he was not known to have engaged in serious theological dialogue with Protestants.

INTERFAITH DIALOGUE

C. Brownlow Hastings, one of the most perceptive and responsible Southern Baptist commentators, works in the denomination's department of interfaith witness. He has written ''A Baptist View of Change in Catholicism,'' iden-

133

tifying developments which Baptists can value positively. In particular, since the Second Vatican Council, Roman Catholic spokesmen describe their Church as ''the people of God,'' not just the priesthood. Bible study is encouraged. Today, some of the easiest cooperation between Roman Catholics and Protestants takes place in the area of biblical research. Mass is no longer said just in Latin. To be sure, Roman Catholic worship is still more liturgical than the low church meeting house practice of most Baptists. No longer regarding the Reformation defensively, a large part of Roman Catholic theologians would say that justification by faith is both biblical and a part of their own tradition.

Denominational leaders report that Baptists who have participated in interfaith activities with them, have learned something about their own faith as well as that of the other party. They have come to be impressed with the all-pervasive character of religion in the life of Roman Catholic believers, as well as the variety which exists beneath labels. Some Roman Catholics, sustained by their own distinctive symbolism and liturgy, exhibit a faith which is not as threatened by modern secularism as that of ''less programmed'' Protestants. Something is learned from them about tradition and community. This is not to say that a Southern Baptist Church is or ought to become a Roman Catholic cathedral. Christians worship sincerely in both types of buildings. Now, Luther's hymn, ''A Mighty Fortress is our God,'' can be sung in Roman Catholic worship. Carter might join in!

James M. Powell, a professor of history at Syracuse University, attempted to view the highly internalized and subjective convictions of Baptist piety against the larger background of Christian history.[6] He suggested that Carter's acceptance address following his nomination, represents ''a millenarian dream in action.'' He relates it to the medieval experience of evangelicalism which dates from as early as the eleventh and twelfth centuries. Movements such as the Lollards and Waldensians radicalized Christian teachings long before the Anabaptists and their counterparts in the Reformation period. Their central message was that individual morality and salvation deserve precedence over priestly hierarchy and church institutions. This theme appears as well in St. Francis of Assisi. Powell describes St. Francis as a truly evangelical spirit, but one who nonetheless submitted to the hierarchy of the Church. It is not surprising that he had difficulty in governing the order he founded; the counsels of perfection do not lead to compromise. Assuredly, a major watershed between Baptists and Roman Catholics is the doctrine of the Church. Baptists reject all hierarchy. Yet different groups of Christians do live in the same world and in the same country.

ROMAN CATHOLICISM AND THE NEW BIRTH

The Southern Baptist historian, James T. Baker, has called attention to the short book by Rosemary Haughton entitled, *The Drama of Salvation*. [7] He urges that the idea of salvation has been often stereotyped in low church piety. Haughton, a Catholic, has concluded that a false dichotomy was created during the Reformation period when theologians on both sides, Roman Catholic and Protestant, looked primarily for differences.

Protestants identified salvation as an act of God—a sudden, often unexpected gift. An "event," it set a person permanently on the road to heaven. Roman Catholic interpretation, by contrast, defined it as the final reward at death for a life of virtue; or at least, it meant dying in sacramental grace. Each party insisted on its own definition in an age of intolerance and polemic. Haughton urges that Catholicism has always believed and taught "Protestant"

135

salvation. Conversion may not be as common as among Southern Baptists, but it does make saints! Baker remarks that the desire for salvation is expressed at Lourdes and Fatima, shrines which attract millions of believers. He points out that "Catholics are sometimes 'saved' too."[8]

For Haughton, the new birth is part of the process of salvation. The designation describes an experience of discontinuity; it seeks to put an event into language through metaphor. Of course, the event is not just a metaphor. Salvation, individually personal, is also celebrated in group worship. God's deed of salvation, his dealing with his people, is the chief subject of the Bible itself. Haughton points out that it belongs to the Old Testament as well as the New Testament. God delivered His people out of their bondage in the land of Egypt.

NEW DIALOGUE?

No doubt, old line Roman Catholics and Southern Baptists have little if anything to discuss with one another. There are significant differences of long standing on such questions as authority and the nature of the Church. Would it be acceptable to say that Roman Catholics and Southern Baptists come to Christianity from different sides of the mountain, as it were? Most members of both parties would find this too tolerant an interpretation. But the fact is that the era of the Counter Reformation has passed. A host of common problems and needs come pouring in on both communions. Older models and antitheses are no longer relevant.

Carter's career has made clear that religion and politics are related, even when there is official separation of church and state. The question is not *whether* they will interact, but *how*. Baptists represent the left wing of the Reformation.

They have not been as clear as many other churches, Roman Catholic or Protestant, about the distinction between secular and sacred, natural and divine law, and what is called "Law and Gospel." Charles Henderson, a Presbyterian, has in mind these differences when he says that Presidents need to be protected from the confusions which are too often a part of their "burden of office."[9] Only as the secular and sacred are seen in their separate functions, he argues, can their subtle connections be properly drawn.

Henderson speaks about "a crazy ambiguity in American opinion about the President." The electorate mistakenly expects him to have a sacerdotal rule, even to be the bringer of salvation. On the one hand, a man of principle is sought, but hope is constantly played off against a deepseated skepticism about the political process. Disappointment is inevitable because the political community is not the place of redemption. Separation of church and state should serve to make this clear. A President may need religion in defeat as well as victory. It can strengthen resolution and integrity as well as provide hope and acceptance in the face of a variety of circumstances. But a dualism between the "city of man" and the "city of God" remains even when there is a sincerely Christian president.

CARTER AND THE JEWS

Carter once said he believes the state of Israel to have been established in fulfillment of Biblical prophecy. The remark reflects an evangelical if not fundamentalist outlook. Paradoxically, some Jews have feared Carter's religion because he is not a religious liberal. In fact, he has been a friend of Israel. As Milton Himmelfarb points out in his article, "Carter and the Jews" in *Commentary,* evangelicals have remained trustworthy supporters of Israel when others have departed.[10]

Robert Shrum, having served very briefly as a Carter speech writer, quoted Carter as saying, "Jackson has all the Jews anyway. I don't get over four percent of the Jewish vote anyway, so forget it. We get the Christians."[11]

Himmelfarb believes most Jews did not understand this as anti-Semitism. It was rather an application of Goldwater's Law: you go hunting for ducks where the ducks are.

Afterward, Carter started hunting for Jewish support and found some. He had made a virtue of being an outsider to Washington. It was there that the Jewish community leaders, concerned for causes such as Israel and civic programs, had connections. Carter was not among them.

Georgia has its own legacy of anti-Semitism. Tom Watson, the Populist, anti-Catholic and racist, was responsible for the only lynching of a Jew in American history, Leo Frank, in 1915. This really has nothing to do with Carter's own good record. He can stand on what he has been and done.

It was to be expected that some Jews would have difficulty in identifying a Protestant, especially a Southern Baptist. Himmelfarb recounts how a young Canadian told him of his bafflement at the University of Toronto. All his life, he had gone to Jewish day schools. At the university, for the first time he encountered schoolmates who were not Jews. They were mainly Scottish, and as Protestants, Presbyterians.

The Jewish student knew what it was to live a Jewish life. A Jew is supposed to eat kosher food, keep the Sabbath, and to pray three times a day wearing *tefillin* on weekday mornings. But what does it mean to live a Presbyterian life? At last he had to ask one of his new friends, "What does a Presbyterian do?" Of course, Baptists are if anything more internalized in their religion than Presbyterians.

CARTER'S DENOMINATION

Carter's denomination is sponsoring excellent materials which give a deeper understanding of Jewish thought and practice. Through interfaith dialogue, Christians can learn much about the background of their own religion. Today, the Southern Baptist Department of Interfaith Witness has much broader concerns than just conversion. The common Baptist belief is that Jews are called of God under the old covenant. Of course, it is important that Judaism and Christianity be understood in their historical background in both similarities and differences. Whatever its limits, the Baptist approach to Jewish life taken by Carter has more authentic depth than a purely secular one. It has similarities with the evangelical faith of the Dutch family, the ten Boons, depicted in the motion picture, *The Hiding Place*.

During the Nazi attacks on synagogues, German Christians came to understand that loyalty to God's own chosen people is a test of authentic Christianity. Carter would understand.

A JEWISH VIEW OF SOUTHERN BAPTISTS

Morris B. Abram wrote on "Governor Carter's Religion" during the election campaign.[12] He reported that growing up Jewish in south Georgia, he had absorbed his share of cruel and scarring words. There were times when he felt threatened, but it was never by the Southern Baptists. They were committed unreservedly to a government divorced from religious coercion. Their deeply felt conviction about the separation of church and state precluded it. Naturally, he knew many evangelicals who hoped that he would embrace Christianity. His conversion would be the natural chain of religious development foretold in the Old Testament. They were puzzled but not angry when he proved incapable of seeing the dazzling light.

Abrams emphasizes: "In such conversations I never felt the need to moderate my views for fear of stronger measures or any form of retribution against me or my family." For forty-five years he lived among Southern Baptists. His maverick status did not deter invitations to speak from their pulpits. He learned the rhythm of their hymns, their folkways, and "most important, the true meaning at the core of their sometimes excessive metaphysical language." In his judgment, "born again" refers to the kind of spiritual awakening that is part of every Western religion.[13]

Michael E. Richmond, Director of the Anti-Defamation League of B'nai Brith in the Chicago area exclaimed: "But in the last analysis, the issue of Carter and Jews is as insubstantial as a cream puff. Bite into it, and there is almost nothing there."[14]

10. Prospects for a Twice-Born President

Jimmy Carter became a ''born again'' Christian more than a decade ago. His autobiography, *Why Not the Best?*, gives no exact date for his conversion experience.[1] It seems to have taken place in 1966 or 1967, and there are at least three versions of what happened. Psychologically, they may be viewed as supplementary rather than contradictory.

The president cites the consequences of his new birth when he is asked about its details. He reports that he became a ''new person, with changed attitudes.'' Not only did he have calm and serenity, he felt able to take defeat with ''complete personal equanimity,'' while still caring for others.

Carter failed in his first attempt to become governor of Georgia, losing the primary election of September, 1966. He was forty-one years old. Defeat came by a narrow margin of only twenty thousand votes in an election in which over a million ballots were cast.

Subsequently, when Carter attended worship at the Plains Baptist Church, he was impressed by a sermon which asked the question, "If you were arrested for being a Christian, would there be enough evidence to convict you?" Carter explains that his attention had centered almost completely on himself. Nothing he undertook to do was gratifying to him, even if successful.

He passed from this very difficult state of life by a "new birth." Realizing that the evidence would not be enough to convict him, he "changed somewhat for the better. I formed a much more intimate relationship with Christ. And since then, I've had just about like a new life. As far as hatreds, frustrations, I feel at ease with myself."

A second account of the conversion experience comes from the president's sister, Ruth Carter Stapleton. Married and the mother of four children, she experienced a period of despair following a serious car accident. Her book, *The Gift of Inner Healing,* explains the peace and joy that came to her from an experience of rebirth.[2] She wished to share it with her brother.

Ruth reports that in the autumn of 1966, they drove from Plains to Webster County and went for a walk in the pine woods.

"I talked about my awareness of Christ, and I shared with Jimmy how it was to come to a place of total commitment, the peace and joy and the power it brings," she says.

She asked her brother if he were willing to give up everything for Christ, even politics.

When he answered in the affirmative, she asked if politics was also included. Ruth warned her brother that until it was, he would be plagued by self-doubt. In the end, his conversion experience brought him peace and serenity.

142

MISSIONARY TRIPS

Her brother's commitment to Christ came to its fulness when he went north to do lay missionary work in Massachusetts and Pennsylvania. Jimmy accepted a pioneer mission assignment as the partner of Milo Pennington, a peanut farmer from Texas. In the late spring of 1967, they went door to door, witnessing to a hundred different families of non-believers, explaining their own faith and seeking conversions. Some fifteen to twenty families accepted Christ. Pennington would fumble verbally, but was effective. Carter felt God's influence and power in their work together.

When he talked with his wife on the telephone, Rosalynn exclaimed, ''Jimmy, you don't sound like the same person. You sound almost like you're intoxicated. . . .''

He replied, ''Well, I am in a way.''

Carter experienced a sense of release, assurance, and peace with himself and with other people. Earlier, individual persons whom he had met seemed unimportant to him. Now he asked what he could do to make ''this other person's life even more enjoyable.''

HIMSELF A BAPTIST

James T. Baker explains that a loosely committed and unenthusiastic Church member reached a new psychological and spiritual nadir. His burden was lifted. ''Putting Jesus first, he went on to be governor of Georgia.''[3]

Baker observes that salvation is a much more common experience among contemporary Americans than many people, even professional theologians, seem to think. He

143

points out that the new birth tends to occur most regularly among those trained by salvationist churches to expect it. Of course this is often in individuals desperately searching for personal recognition, fulfillment, and security.

"But all in all it's a perfectly natural experience that answers perfectly normal needs," he concludes.

Theologically, it means calling upon God and believing He responds, or better, it is being called by God and responding. Conversion as a stunning act of God at a specific time in a person's life is often stereotyped in low church Protestantism, Baker observes. But in defense he adds that it occurs widely and without being programmed. The Roman Catholic sociologist, Father Andrew Greeley, has shown in his research that a considerable part of the population has had a religious experience, often one of conversion.

THE BAPTIST INTERPRETATION OF CONVERSION

Jimmy Carter as a Southern Baptist is, of course, a specific kind of saved person in his conversion. For his tradition, salvation is identified as a freely and inevitably offered gift of God, open to all who accept it. Conversion comes about through "conviction," when the Word of God is preached. Without it, church membership is meaningless and empty. Conversion is often accompanied by significant emotion, and brings a change of lifestyle; this is the case especially with adults.

Among children reaching the age of responsibility, religious experience is expected before the individual can be baptized and enjoy the full privileges of church membership.

Like Carter, the first conversion experience of grace can be followed in later years by a second, usually much deeper experience. Baker says that the latter may be interpreted in two ways: either as a sign that the person was not really "saved" before, or as a return to or a deepening of faith. The second type of experience sometimes leads to charismatic "signs of the Spirit." Generally, Southern Baptists discourage faith healing and speaking in tongues. Ruth Carter Stapleton seems to have felt a special sense of mission and a new healing ministry. In the president's case, the results flowed into his political career.

Baker concludes Jimmy Carter's "salvation experience" seems about as healthy as possible. It was the kind that enlightened Southern Baptist ministers encourage. Carter concluded, "God wants me to be the best politician I can possibly be." The second birth gave him inner peace without neutralizing his ambition. It has made him something of a social reformer—but with a sense of love. He was not verbally radical, and has been able to continue to work with his Southern constituency.

Two members of the faculty at the Massachusetts Institute of Technology, Bruce Mazlish, Chairman of the History Department whose work we have already cited, and a senior lecturer in Political Science, Edwin Diamond, have attempted an analysis of the president's second birth. They observe that "while words may come hard for Carter, we believe he has made the born-again experience accessible and understandable, even for non-believers."[4] In Baptist theology, the new birth is highly moral. The believer receives God's mercy and is released from a sense of sin, and the convert is reborn to new life in the Spirit. All earlier personality traits do not disappear, but through the love of Christ, they are brought under His Lordship and control.

SEQUENCE OF EVENTS

As a work of grace, conversion cannot be reduced to its experiential components. None the less they remain important. Carter's experience came in the aftermath of his defeat in the first race for governor. It was natural at such a time that he would ask existentially about life's purpose. This kind of crisis is common in middle life. It raises such questions as what one has created and what legacy he will leave to posterity. How can old age be faced with integrity and assurance? Carter's conversion has been described as an inward validation of selfish desires together with their transformation.

It began when Carter, defeated politically, felt a sense of being a hypocrite and lacked peace. Carter's description of his state, offered in a conversation with Bill Moyers, showed phenomena common for this stage of life. He spoke of always thinking about himself and an inability to love. In other words, he experienced depression and narcissism. Reflecting on his own shortcomings and sinfulness, Carter felt filled with pride, regretted that he had used people, and expressed a need to reform. Erik Erikson, who has researched the experiences of Luther and Ghandi, identifies the pattern as "crisis of generativity."[5] Through his rebirth, Carter was assured of his own inherent goodness and worth. Accepting God the Father through Christ, he in turn came to know that he was accepted by the Father.

Carter's missionary work reinforced his experience of new birth. The former nuclear submarine officer, Annapolis graduate, candidate for governor, well-educated and proud of his achievement, went door to door in Lock Haven, Pennsylvania. His self-image was that of a scientist and man of culture.

By contrast, Carter's companion was a man poorly educated and in his seventies. Carter saw that the old fumbler, doing the talking, succeeded. He asked why? What had science, reason, and intellect brought Carter? He had been unable to win the election, but old Pennington was able to reach people and to convert them.

Already in Georgia politics, Carter had come to learn that the range of his outreach was determined by the power that he could exercise. While state senator, he had fought selfish interests as they attempted to mislead good, but ordinary people. To do more, he would have to become governor and then president.

The Protestant character of the president's experience is apparent. "Jimmy Carter's identification with people, we believe, is a mystical union (as was his union with God). There are no intermediaries."[6]

This premise explains why Carter invites people to become part of his family. During the early part of his presidential campaign, he lived in their houses. He says he does not want to create issues but wishes to learn what concerns the people most deeply. It was a new Jimmy Carter who was elected Georgia governor in 1970.

Events indicate Carter's personal crisis began soon after his return from the Navy. His father's death was one of the few occasions, his sister Ruth recalls, when she ever saw her brother cry. Together, they went out to notify the people of the town.

"We started out early in the morning. We went to black and white." To their surprise, they learned the senior Carter had supplemented the income of many families of both races, helping also to pay college expenses.

As the young Carter began to review his life, comparing it with that of his father, he exclaimed, "I want to be a man like him."

Actually, Jimmy had seen little of his father from 1942 to 1953. Feelings of guilt and redemption were natural. Even after he had become a successful farmer, business man, Sunday School teacher and state legislator, the persistence of a sense of failure seems to be related to the figure of Jimmy's father. The older man had been an exuberant person, like Jimmy's brother, Billy. Billy, a college drop-

147

out, but a "good ole boy," knew how to relax and take defeat. Jimmy was too proud and selfish to do so. His twice-born experience meant that he was accepted by God the Father. Politics in his new style came with his sense of redemption, enabling him to express the love that supports and brings self-esteem.

In the end, a conversion experience gave the man who was later to become president both a new self and a vision of the American citizen. Without a new birth experience, he would have remained an Active/Negative character, to use Barber's terms. It was through his conversion experience that he learned to accept failure, admit mistakes, and to love others. There still may be regressions; sometimes he may be prideful. However, Carter has become a mature person of serenity with a sense of community that communicates itself readily to the public. He does care.

CARTER AND NIXON

Mazlish and Diamond note that some people, "to take the scariest concern," find that Carter seems to look like Nixon. Each has the liberal mother and conservative father. Nixon's conversion experience reportedly occurred in his fourteenth year at a revival meeting in Los Angeles to which he had been taken by his father. Both men are tenacious, talk much about roots, work hard, and reassure audiences of their honesty. Nixon said, "I'm not a crook." Carter says, "I will never lie to you."

Mazlish and Diamond find that these supposed resemblances are superficial and possibly misleading as well. Nixon talked religion but there is little evidence that he was guided by it. President Carter really does have roots. "He moves *out* from the South, not *away* from it."[7] Driving seven miles down the macadam road from his home, he can show the family gravestones dating from the 1800's. Nixon's image of his father, unlike that of Carter, was that of a failure. The son's anger and hate were so deep and threatening that he had to deny their existence completely, never coming to terms with them. Psychologically rigid and eternally dissatisfied with accomplishments, he seemed almost inevitably headed for disaster.

Carter's religion and ambition are tied together in his conversion experience. Faith in God is related to his deepest motivation for responsible participation in political life. He accepts the Christian value system, and he is not tired or worn out in seeking to reach what he conceives to be its goals.

For the new president, God is not dead! Beyond any achievement, he has an eschatological vision of a goodness which is more than his own, a judgment which he cannot pronounce finally. In the last analysis, the future is in God's hands, although at present men have great freedom and responsibility.

PROSPECTS OF THE CARTER PRESIDENCY

Neil R. Peirce interviewed Carter twice before writing "A Preview of a Jimmy Carter Presidency" for the *Los Angeles Times*. Peirce concluded:

The style and thrust of a Jimmy Carter Presidency would startle the nation—and jolt official Washington—as profoundly as the Georgian's meteoric rise from obscurity to capture the Democratic party nomination.[8]

Whether Carter can succeed in fulfilling his bold promises remains to be seen, Pierce thinks. But there can be no question about the president's immense energy and drive, not just to attain office, but to use it to carry out his programs.

Peirce finds Carter's sometimes coldly calculating personal ambition is joined to an elevated vision of what a president could do to transform the shape of American society. Assuredly, it has religious roots in his second birth.

THE POLITICS OF LOVE

Harold Straughn, writing in *Mission* magazine, has made a speculative, optimistic analysis of the president's politics of love.[9] After Vietnam and Watergate, Straughn observes, cynicism usurped the place of love as a catalyst to power and justice. He proposes that Carter's new metaphysics of the center is based on love. It moves into what is often viewed as a wasteland by both activists and theoretists.

Straughn attempts to justify his conclusion from Paul Tillich's short book, entitled *Love, Power and Justice*.[10] Tillich, whom Carter has quoted on a number of occasions, is one of the few thinkers to take love seriously as a political reality. German in background, he attempted to work out an ontological view of these three forces in political life.

Tillich discusses what happens to a society where power and justice exist without love. Justice defined as zeal for reform becomes polarized against power, defined as technological and military growth. In America, the left has often thought that energy comes from pursuit of justice while the right has understood its legitimacy to be based on defense of authority. Love alone can bind together the left and right, justice and power, in mutual interdependence. Suspicion and mutual exclusiveness are minimized. At the same time, politically, love is a movement toward openness and vulnerability, away from secrecy and the inability to trust people. A back and forth movement of mutual relations is nurtured and improved. Policy is not enacted once and for all without change and review.

Love comes into politics not only as hope but also as risk. The risk is that men have lost the ability to trust or to care. There is also the risk that love will degenerate into a cover for sentimentality, nostalgia, idealism for zeal without knowledge, and form without substance. But a strategy of love can have practical consequences; it can make things work. The right can stimulate respect before an array of might. The left can stimulate outrage at injustice. Love means that the polarity between them needs to be deepened at another level. The center which it establishes is more than a compromise, concensus, or mere coalition. It is dynamic, an expanding universe in which love holds left and right together, radiating outward. Straughn urges that it has a pluralism at its core like an atom containing negative and positive charges. Left and right are both correct when they get the impression that the center is moving toward them. It seems to be radiating out in all directions at once, not just toward one part alone.

POLITICAL REALITIES

The question of the relation of love, power, and justice is an all-important one. Characteristically, low church Protestants, the second wave of the Reformation, have emphasized love. Does it really have the integrating effect Straughn assigns to it? How will love stand up in a wicked world? William Lee Miller notes in partial endorsement that the president is not naive about the prevalence of self-interest in collective life. He knows about "the effects of nuclear proliferation, the Russians, the hard blows of politics, the complexities of public administration."[11]

Garry Wills remarks: "Those who complain of Carter's

151

cold eyes would be just as upset if he were a wild-eyed hot-gospeler.'' President Carter likes order and sometimes creates it ruthlessly. As a California assemblyman remarked at the Democratic National Convention: ''You cash no loser's tickets at Jimmy Carter's window.''[12]

Carter's achievement has been phenomenal, coming from obscurity to the presidency in scarcely a year's time. Now, the tasks before him are enormous. President Hesburgh of Notre Dame University has written: ''That person should be the next president who has a great vision of what America can be in the years ahead.''[13]

The post-Watergate situation is one in which the reality of evil in the national life has become very clear—from the break-in itself, Vietnam, domestic poverty and inflation. It is not hard to understand why some idealists have refused participation in public life. Yet democracy cannot live or prosper from such a response. Political evil feeds on the inaction of good people.

At the opposite extreme are the instant activists, still expecting that everything can be accomplished at once. Normal political processes are to be cut around in impatience. Both positions lack depth! President Carter knows as well the emotional pietism which seeks only personal salvation, believing that good men will make a good society. Its result was to leave the field for the Haldemans and Ehrlichmans. Religiously motivated persons need to become involved politically, refusing as well, ''paralysis by analysis.'' Carter, at least, has been a man of action.

Paradoxically, an interesting result may follow from Carter's explicit Christian commitment. The president shares the recognition that faith in God has been an important factor in American culture—but this does not necessarily mean uniformity. As governor, Carter adhered to the line of separation between church and state very carefully. For him, the American nation under God is a political commonwealth, not the ultimate community. Too often, patriotic, national symbols have received the devotion that should go more fully to God alone. Popular piety, spread so freely in the nation's capital, has lacked profundity. An indirect result of Carter's understanding of Christian faith could be that his presidency would help rid American governmental life of religious sentimentality and display.

RELIGION AND CIVILIZATION

The English historian, Arnold Toynbee, has described religion with the figure of a chariot which outlasts civilizations, carrying human life ever higher. More enduring than governments and nations, faith in God provides the creative basis for culture. Can it be that a new sensitivity to this role is reflected in President Carter's rise to prominence and power? We have concluded that he belongs to the mainstream of the American dream, with a sound, healthy religious common sense. For him, religion is not just an outsider to American civilization. His deepest roots are not secular, but in the Hebrew-Christian legacy.

Too often, in the era of the two world wars, civilization has experienced a polarity between "breadth" and "depth." Persons or outlooks of tolerance and universal outreach have been disastrously ineffective. Others with conviction in depth, parochial if not fanatical—the Hitlers and Stalins—have determined the course of events. The tragic result has been evident in man's inhumanity to man. By contrast, it is characteristic of high religion that it joins depth and breadth profoundly. Christianity, for example, gives human life an inclusive context. Can it be that Carter's religion shares this double aspect?

There is no assurance that the threat of nihilism, ending in nuclear destruction, is past. The possibility of hydrogen warfare remains. At the same time, the most fundamental values of civilization are at stake in the struggle for the dignity and worth of human beings. In such a context, politics as usual is no longer possible.

If America can offer only scientism and self-interest, it will have little chance of capturing the imagination of mankind for its dream of democracy and tolerance. Freedom and personal development go together—but freedom for what? The president's answer is that politics is not an end in itself. In the words of his sister, "You've got to look beyond yourself for God's purpose. You've got to be less self-centered in all of your life."[14]

Footnotes

PREFACE

1. April 1976, interview. *Cf.*, Robert L. Turner, *"I'll Never Lie to You,"* *Jimmy Carter in his Own Words* (New York: Ballantine, 1976), 83.
2. Nashville, October 1975.
3. Howard Norton and Bob Slosser, *The Miracle of Jimmy Carter* (Plainfield, New Jersey: Logos, 1976), 13.
4. Leslie Wheeler, *Jimmy Who?* (Woodbury, New York: Barron's, 1976), 11.
5. Interview with Bill Moyers, May 6, 1976, 39. *Cf.*, Wheeler, *op. cit.*, 11.
6. *Why Not the Best*, 59.
7. *Ibid.*, 57.
8. Norton and Slosser, 25.
9. Martin Schram, *Running for President, A Journal of the Carter Campaign* (New York: Pocket Books, 1976), 65.
10. Norton and Slosser, 57.
11. Schram, *op. sit.*, 11.

CHAPTER 1

1. *New York* magazine, March 22, 1976, 30.
2. *New York Times,* September 28, 1976, 29.
3. *New York* magazine, May 24, 1976, 12.
4. Charles P. Henderson, Jr., "The Politics of Love," *Nation,* May 8, 1976, 554.

5. *Commonweal,* July 1, 1976, 430.
6. Interview with Kim Watson, *Baptist Home Mission,* April 1974.
7. *Ms.,* October 1976, 88.
8. "Plains Truth," *Atlantic Monthly,* June 1976, 49-54.
9. Henderson, *op. cit.*
10. Matthew 22:21.
11. Alexander Solzhenitsyn, *Gulag Archipelago I* (Glasgow: Collins, 1974), 611-612.
12. *New York Times,* September 28, 1976, 30.
13. "Niceguyin' His Way to the White House?" *National Review,* May 14, 1976, 502.
14. *Ibid.,* 503.
15. *Ibid.,* 502.
16. *Ibid.,* 504.
17. *New York* magazine, May 24, 1976, 12.
18. "Plains Truth," *Atlantic Monthly,* June 1976, 51.
19. *Cf., Thus Spake Zarathustra.*
20. Robert Coles, "Jimmy Carter, Agrarian Rebel," *New Republic,* June 26, 1976, 19.
21. *Ibid.*
22. *Playboy,* November 1976, 84.
23. Norton and Slosser, 89.
24. "Three Strands of Jimmy Carter's Religion," *New Republic,* June 6, 1976, 15-17.
25. Ed., Harry R. Davis and Robert C. Good (New York: Scribners, 1960).
26. August 7, 1976, 40.
27. Mailer, *New York Times,* September 28, 1976, 76.
28. Cited by Clare Booth Luce, "The Light at the End of the Tunnel of Love," *National Review,* November 12, 1976, 1228.
29. *Cf.,* back cover of Schram, *op. cit.*
30. "The Politics of Love," *Nation,* May 8, 1976, 555.
31. *Ibid.,* 556.
32. Luce, *op. cit.,* 1228.
33. "Jimmy Carter and the Democratic Crisis," *New Republic,* July 3 & 10, 1976, 19.

34. Holifield, *op. cit.,* 15.

CHAPTER 2
1. "Thinking Aloud," *The Tie,* October-November 1976, 12.
2. *Ibid.*
3. *Cf.,* Sydney E. Ahlstrom, *A Religious History of the American People* (New Haven: Yale, 1972), 81.
4. *Ibid.,* 170.
5. Morris B. Abram, "Governor Carter's Religion," *Nation,* September 25, 1976, 261.
6. *Cf.,* C. Dwight Dorough, *The Bible Belt Mystique* (Philadelphia: Westminster, 1974), 1.
7. *Ibid.,* 31.
8. *Ibid.,* 32.
9. *Ibid.*
10. *Ibid.,* 197.
11. *Ibid.,* 188.
12. Comment in a personal interview with the author.
13. *World Mission Journal,* October 1974, 3.
14. Norton and Slosser, 92-93.

CHAPTER 3
1. "God and the 1976 Election," *Wall Street Journal,* April 28, 1976, 18.
2. Natick, W. A. Wilde Company, 1961.
3. Ahlstrom, *op. cit.,* 366.
4. Leo Pfeffer, *Church, State and Freedom* (Boston: Beacon Press, 1967), 104-105.
5. *Ibid.,* 91.
6. *Ibid.,* 96.
7. *Ibid.,* 103.
8. *Ibid.,* 107.
9. *Cf.,* Paul F. Boller, Jr., *George Washington and Religion* (Dallas: Southern Methodist University Press, 1963), 118.
10. *Ibid.,* 156.
11. *Ibid.,* 95.
12. Cited by Robert N. Bellah, "Civil Religion in America," *Daedalus,* Winter, 1967, 1.

13. Pfeffer, *op. cit.*, 105.
14. *Ibid.*
15. To S. Kercheval, Monticello, January 19, 1810. Cited by Adrienne Koch, *The Philosophy of Thomas Jefferson* (Gloucester: Massachusetts, Pater Smith, 1957), 26.
16. To Dr. Benjamin Rush, Washington, April 21, 1803. Koch, *op. cit.*, 31.
17. Bellah, *op. cit.*, 2.
18. *Ibid.*, 3-4.
19. *Ibid.*, 7-8.
20. New York: Harper, 1973.
21. "The Religion of Abraham Lincoln," in Allan Nevins (ed.), *Lincoln and the Gettysburg Address* (Urbana: Illinois, 1964), 72.
22. Bellah, *op. cit.*, 1.'
23. "God, Caesar, and the People," *National Review,* September 3, 1976, 956.
24. Boller, *op. cit.*, 46-47.

CHAPTER 4

1. Wheeler, *op. cit.*, 105.
2. Houston: Gulf Publishing Company, 1976, 278.
3. New York: Dell, 1975, 409.
4. New York: Simon and Schuster, 1976, 422.
5. Charles P. Henderson, Jr., *The Nixon Theology* (New York: Harper, 1972), 3.
6. *Ibid.*, 2.
7. *Ibid.*, 193.
8. Bruce Mazlish, *In Search of Nixon* (New York: Basic Books, 1972).
9. Erwin C. Hargrove, *The Power of the Modern Presidency* (Philadelphia: Temple University Press, 1974), 17.
10. Englewood Cliffs, New Jersey: Prentice Hall, 1972, 17.
11. *Ibid.*, 450.
12. *Ibid.*, 454.

CHAPTER 5

1. S. J. Ungar, "How Jimmy Carter Does It," *Atlantic Monthly,* July 1976, 33.

2. *Why Not the Best?*, 36.
3. K. Bode, "Why Carter's Big with Blacks," *New Republic*, April 10, 1976, 14.
4. *Why Not the Best?*, 33.
5. Turner, *op. cit.*, 104.
6. *Christianity Today*, "Carter's Background," October 8, 1976, 42.
7. Joseph C. Hough, Jr., *Black Power and White Protestants* (New York, 1968), 86.
8. *Ibid.*, 89.
9. Bode, *op. cit.*, 14.
10. *Ibid.*
11. Orde Coombs, "Blacks and Rednecks: The Holy Alliance of '76," *New York* magazine, July 19, 1976, 57.
12. Julian Bond, "Why I Don't Support Jimmy Carter," *Nation*, April 17, 1976, 454-455.
13. Coles, *op. cit.*, 17.
14. tr. Olive Wyon, London, Allen and Unwin, 1931, 55 *et seq.*
15. *Cf.*, *New York* magazine, July 19, 1976, 61.
16. Coles, *op. cit.*, 17.
17. *Ibid.*

CHAPTER 6

1. *Playboy, op. cit.*, 77.
2. *Ibid.*, 74.
3. *Ibid.*
4. *Ibid.*
5. Henderson, *The Nixon Theology*, 168.
6. *Playboy, op. cit.*, 70.
7. Cited by Henderson, *The Nixon Theology*, 131.
8. *Ibid.*
9. *Ibid.*, 170.
10. Bruce Mazlish, *Kissinger, The European Mind in American Policy* (New York, 1976), 12.
11. *Ibid.*, 285.
12. *Ibid.*
13. *Ibid.*
14. *Ibid.*, 293.
15. *Ibid.*, 269.

16. "Carter's Foreign Policy," *New Republic,* July 17, 1976, 14-16.
17. Mazlish, *Kissinger,* 294.
18. *Time,* August 2, 1976, 13.
19. George McKenna, *American Populism* (New York: Putnam, 1974), xxiii.
20. *Ibid.,* p. 22.
21. Henderson, "The Politics of Love," 556.
22. James Burnham, "Politics and Morality," *National Review,* November 12, 1976, 1226.
23. *Time,* November 15, 1976, 24.
24. *Ibid.*
25. Schram, *op. cit.,* i.

CHAPTER 7

1. Playboy, *op. cit.,* 86.
2. *Newsweek,* October 4, 1976, 70.
3. *Ibid.,* 71.
4. *Time,* October 4, 1976, 34.
5. *Ibid.*
6. *Ibid.*
7. *Wall Street Journal,* October 18, 1976, 24.
8. *Christian Century,* October 6, 1976, 847.
9. *New Republic,* October 9, 1976, 18.
10. *Ibid.,* 19.
11. First edition, 1910.
12. Davis and Good, *op. cit.,* 19.

CHAPTER 8

1. *Cf.,* David Kucharsky, *The Man from Plains* (New York: Harper, 1976), 23.
2. *Ibid.*
3. Richard Quebedeaux, *The Young Evangelicals* (New York: Harper, 1974), 4.
4. *Newsweek,* October 25, 1976, 68.
5. Holifield, *op. cit.,* 16.
6. *Ibid.*
7. *Newsweek, op. cit.,* 75.

8. *Ibid.*, 76.
9. Quebedeaux, *op. cit.*, 35.
10. *Ibid.*
11. *Ibid.*, 13.
12. *Op. cit., Atlantic Monthly,* June 1976.
13. Quebedeaux, *op. cit.*, 8-9.
14. *Ibid.*, 14.
15. *Newsweek, op. cit.*, 76.
16. Grand Rapids: Zondervan.
17. Kucharsky, *op. cit.*, 49.
18. *Cf.,* Mailer, *op. cit.*, 76.
19. Davis and Good, *op. cit.*, 205.
20. Philadelphia and New York: Lippincott, 1972.

CHAPTER 9
1. Mailer, *op. cit.*, 73.
2. *National Catholic Reporter,* September 24, 1976, 20.
3. *Ibid.*, September 10, 1976, 17.
4. *Cf., Christian Century,* October 13, 1976, 853-854.
5. Robert F. Drinan, "Governor Carter's Commitment to Christian Concerns,"*America,* October 30, 1976, 270-272.
6. *America,* October 23, 1976, 249-250.
7. Baker, *op. cit.*, (Haughton, New York: Seabury Press, 1975).
8. *Ibid.*
9. Henderson, "The Politics of Love," 557.
10. Milton Himmelfarb, "Carter and the Jews," *Commentary,* August 1976, 48.
11. Schram, *op. cit.*, 157-160.
12. Abram, *op. cit.*
13. *Ibid.*
14. "Carter and the Jews," *Christian Century,* October 26, 1976, 928.

CHAPTER 10
1. Turner, *op. cit.*, 79.
2. Waco, Word, 1976.
3. Baker, *op. cit.*

4. "Thrice-Born, A Psychohistory of Jimmy Carter's Re-birth," *New York* magazine, August 30, 1976, 26-33.
5. Erik H. Erikson, *Young Man Luther, A Study in Psychoanalysis and History* (New York: Norton, 1961). Recent statements by the president and his wife indicate that they believe the turmoil of the period following his defeat in his first race for governor has been overstated (*Cf.* Time, January 10, 1977, p. 12).
6. Mazlish and Diamond, 30.
7. *Ibid.*
8. *Los Angeles Times,* July 18, 1976.
9. *Mission* magazine, Austin, Texas, October 1976, 7-9.
10. New York: Oxford University Press, 1954.
11. Miller, *New Republic, op. cit.,* 18.
12. "The Carter Question," *New York Review of Books,* August 5, 1976, 21.
13. *Worldview,* January/February 1976, 3.
14. Norton and Slosser, 30.

3   4028   09897   8613

HARRIS COUNTY PUBLIC LIBRARY